Contents

Acknowledgements

The author wishes to thank:

The young writers: Rahila Ahmed, Joanna Craig, Julia Crossland, Helen Davies, Marie-Anne Everett, Matthew Gaunt, Simone Gerraghty, Terri Gill, Eleanor Harper, Carla Immerson, Richard Jeffrey, John Jennings, Russell Jones, Romany Kershaw, Balvinder Kaur, Popinder Kaur, Claire Lewis, William Lewis, Kirstie Moran, Oliver Neil, Richard Pasco, James Porter, Jennie Roberts, Rowena Smith, James Smith, Tamsin Suitor, Mark Taylor, Thomas Turner, Adrian Tuplin, Remina Walsh, Daniel Watts and Alice Wright, for permission to include their work.

The teachers: Patricia Campbell, Janet Evans, Maureen Johnson, Jayne Morrison, Sue Nelson, Christine Phinn, Carl Prescott, Simon Peace, David Reece, Jacky Roberts and Helen Shepherd for their cooperation and support.

The bookseller, Sonia Benster of the Children's Bookshop, Lindley, Huddersfield for her invaluable advice and recommendations.

My editor, John Owens, for his encouragement and advice.

My family: Christine, my wife and our four children for their patience and understanding.

My son: Matthew Phinn, in particular, for the illustrations.

Preface

In a speech to the Conservative Party Conference on Friday 8 October 1993, the then Prime Minister, John Major, stated that: 'Unless we teach a child to read, we hobble that child for the rest of his life.' No parent, employer, educational pundit or newspaper editor would, of course, argue with that. Reading is the fundamental tool for all learning. Reading opens doors. Reading is the very key to knowledge. No teacher would disagree with John Major either. She might not find the word 'hobble' – to tie together the legs to prevent escape – the most appropriate of metaphors to use, but would be the first to concede that a person unable to read is disabled and that the teaching of reading is the single most important task in early years education. The present Prime Minister and his Secretary of State also have much to say about the importance of reading, and primary schools have seen yet more upheavals in the curriculum to accommodate a greater emphasis on the teaching of literacy skills.

Given the increased importance ascribed to literacy in schools, this book seeks to offer teachers practical and readable advice for ways in which they might respond and adapt their practice to take account of the new curricular requirements. The text is, above all, a practical handbook, offering teachers suggestions and strategies which I hope they will find useful as they grapple with the challenges posed by the implementation of the Literacy Strategy and the introduction of the Literacy Hour. It also provides a resource not merely to help children to read but to help them to become keen, discriminatory, lifelong readers and lovers of books.

Gervase Phinn
Doncaster
December 1999

Introduction

The people who want higher literacy standards most are primary teachers. They know more than anyone the joy of watching a child grasp the skills of reading; of seeing a child find out about the real world, and many imaginary ones too, through books.

(Barber 1998)

'Are you here to hear me read ?' The speaker was Helen, a healthy-looking little girl of six with long golden plaits, wide unblinking eyes and a face as speckled as a thrush's egg. I met her when I was listening to children read in a small village primary school some years ago.

'That's right,' I replied, 'Here to hear you read.'

'I'm a very good reader you know.'

'Really?'

'I use expression.'

'You probably use dramatic pause as well,' I said smiling and staring into the large pale eyes.

'I don't know what it is,' she said pertly, 'but I probably do.' Helen did, in fact, read with great fluency, expression and confidence. She paused dramatically in her reading. 'I *am* a good reader, aren't I?'

'No,' I said mischievously. 'You're not.'

'I am,' she said firmly.

'You are the best reader I think I have ever heard,' I told her.

'I'm very good at writing as well,' she commented casually when she snapped the book shut.

'Really?'

'Would you care to see my writing?'

'I would love to,' I said.

'Poetry or prose?'

'Poetry please.'

'I have my poems in a portfolio.'

'I guessed you would,' I replied, chuckling. Helen's writing was as confident and as clear as her reading. 'And why are you such a good reader?' I asked.

'Because I read a lot,' she said simply. 'And I love books.'

Helen then told me about her favourite authors and poets and how, from the earliest age, the adults in her life – Mummy, Daddy, Granny and Grampa – had sat her on their knees, read to her, told her stories, talked about books, taken her to the library and to the bookshop, bought her books for Christmas and her birthday and helped her build up her own collection of books in her bedroom. In the evening there was a quiet time when everyone in the house read. Of course, it should come as no surprise that Helen was a highly competent, confident and keen reader. She had been raised in that rich, motivating reading environment where books are important and valued; an environment which produces the lifelong reader. This, of course, is the key to reading. As Jane Shilling writes: 'If a child is to learn to love reading, it needs to be presented as a natural, essential pleasure, not as a duty.' She continues to describe the environment in which her own son, a voracious reader, is reared – an environment, like Helen's, 'entirely permeated with narrative':

> I certainly did not set out to create a precocious reader. There are in our house no early reader systems designed to inveigle unwary toddlers into premature literacy, not even those little board books containing emasculated versions of more complex texts. What I did was to read to him, nightly, from the moment he came home from hospital, aged three days. I read the books I liked as a child – 'Beatrix Potter', 'Orlando, the Marmalade Cat', 'The Wind in the Willows', Ralph Caldecott's books of poetry, and so on.

She concludes her article with some sensible advice for parents:

> Surround a child with books from birth, make them as ordinary a part of his life as knives and forks and plates, present reading as an activity as natural and essential as breathing, and at seven years or so, you will have your reward – the singular semi-silence broken only by heavy breathing, an occasional half laugh, and the regular swish of a turning page that is the sound of your child setting off to explore new worlds whose only boundaries are the covers of his book.
>
> (Shilling 1999)

It has, of course, been ever thus. The poet Coleridge wrote of his childhood:

> I read every book that came my way without distinction – and my father was very fond of me, and used to take me on his knee, and hold long conversations with me. I remember, that at eight years old, I walked with him one winter evening from a farmer's house, a mile from Ottery – and he told me the names of the stars – and how Jupiter was a thousand times larger than our world and that the other twinkling stars were suns that had worlds rolling around them – and when I came home, he shewed me how they rolled round. I heard him with profound delight and admiration; but without the least mixture of wonder or incredulity. For from my early reading of Faery Tales, and Genii etc. etc. – my mind had been habituated to the Vast.
>
> (Holmes 1990)

This is what teachers should be about – habituating children to the vastness of literature. Schools should be for all children, and particularly for those in homes where there are few if any books and little if any importance placed on reading, what the home is for the most fortunate children like Helen. They should provide an environment for reading where children are exposed to material which arouses their interest in, and develops a love of reading. They should be cheerful, optimistic, welcoming places where children are surrounded with language and presented with a rich and stimulating variety of stories, poems, plays and non-fiction material which will make them smile and laugh, be captivated and curious, sometimes feel sad and a little scared and which will encourage them to want more and more and more.

PART I

Treasure

Opening the covers of a book
Is like lifting the lid of a treasure chest.
Look inside and you will find
Golden stories and glittering characters.

Some are given a map to show them where X marks the spot,
Some are given the precious key to open up the lock,
Some are helped to lift the heavy lid,
But for some it will remain a buried treasure.

Gervase Phinn

Chapter 1
Choosing Books for Children

What are needed are beginning texts that fascinate children and convince them that reading is delightful and helps one to gain a better understanding of oneself and others – in short, of the world we live in and how to live in it. To achieve this, primary texts should stimulate and enrich the child's imagination, as fairy tales do, and should develop the child's literary sensitivities, as good poems are apt to do. The texts should also present the child with literary images of the world, of nature and of man, as these have been created by great writers.

(Bettelheim and Zelan 1982)

There cannot be a teacher in the country who would not subscribe to this view or who would not dispute the recommendations contained in the National Curriculum and in the National Literacy Strategy:

Teaching should cover a range of rich and stimulating texts and should ensure that pupils regularly hear stories, told or read aloud, and hear and share poetry read by the teacher and each other...Reading should include picture books, nursery rhymes, poems, folk tales, myths, legends and other literature. Both boys and girls should experience a wide range of children's literature.

(DES 1989)

In the early stages, pupils should have a carefully balanced programme of guided reading from books of graded difficulty, matched to their independent reading levels. These guided reading books should have a cumulative vocabulary, sensible grammatical structure and a lively and interesting content. Through shared reading, pupils should also be given a rich experience of more challenging texts.

(DfEE 1998b)

Teachers know that to become as successful a reader as Helen, children have to be familiar with and use a range of strategies to understand the text and need the support and encouragement of sensitive and enthusiastic adults to develop the love of books. They also know that the provision of a wide range of good quality texts is essential. These principles are at the heart of the National Curriculum and the National Literacy Strategy and have formed the basis for the successful teaching and encouragement of reading for many many years. But where does the teacher start? What books in particular should be presented to children? Which material is appropriate? What are the qualities of 'a good book'?

Before selecting books for the young reader there are a number of questions one should ask:

- Is the book visually appealing and eye-catching? Picture books with bright, colourful and beautifully illustrated covers demand to be picked up and read.
- Is the subject appropriate to the children in terms of age and maturity? Does it avoid being moralistic, overly sentimental and patronising? Does it portray class, gender and culture in an unstereotypical way?
- Is the story worth telling? Does it read well aloud and bear a rereading? Is it entertaining and challenging? Does it contain some excitement and suspense? Does it kindle curiosity and imagination?

C. S. Lewis argued vehemently that:

No book is really worth reading at the age of ten which is not equally worth reading at the age of fifty – except of course information books. The only imaginative works we ought to grow out of are those which it would be better not to have read at all.

(Lewis in Meek 1977)

- Is the language appropriate, natural and meaningful? Does it encourage children to predict what will happen, to anticipate and become involved in the narrative? Is there a richness in the expression and an imaginative use of words? Does the writer make some demands on his or her readers in terms of language? Good books expose a child to language in its most complex and varied forms, presenting the thoughts, emotions and experiences of others in a vivid and dramatic way.

> Aesthetic properties of language are to be found more than anywhere in literature. Literature is nothing if not language formed in highly deliberate ways. From the earliest preschool stages of development, children are interested in forms of language. Wide reading, and as great an experience as possible of the best imaginative literature, are essential to the full development of an ear for language.
>
> (DES 1988a)

- Is the dialogue appropriate to the characters? Is it clear, authentic and under-standable? Does it capture the rhythms of speech? Does it reflect the speech patterns of those for whom it is intended?
- Do the illustrations enhance the story, adding meaning to the words rather than detracting from them? Do the pictures link closely to the text? 'All early reading material should be attractive not only in presentation but in content. The words and pictures should complement each other in such a way that the child needs to examine both with equal care.' (DES 1975)
- Is the print clear, well-spaced and of an appropriate size?
- Are the characters rounded and convincing? Do they live and breath on the page, develop and grow in the reader's mind? Can children readily identify with the characters and enter into their lives?
- Is the story by a real writer, not merely a book especially written to teach children to read? 'Authors who genuinely want to write for children do not count the words in a sentence. They know instinctively where phrases start and stop because they shape narratives and incidents.' (Meek 1982)
- Is the story of real interest to the teacher? Does she enjoy reading and rereading it, presenting it and discussing it with her children?

Recommended stories

Here are four good stories:

1. Amy Said *by Martin Waddell, illustrated by Charlotte Voake (Reception/Year 1)*

Martin Waddell has written many fine books for younger readers and all have enormous appeal. His stories are wonderfully warm and sympathetic and capture the imagination of children as well as enhancing their linguistic abilities. *Amy Said* is an original and compelling short story: funny, bright and full of happy life and movement. It has lively language, lots of repetition and a robust little character whose actions delight young children. Big sister Amy is an expert about what to do at Gran's house and she gets her little brother into a whole lot of bother.

> When Amy and I stayed with Gran,
> I wanted to bounce on my bed
> and Amy said I could.
> I bounced a bit,
> then a bit more,
> then bit more.
> Then I fell off the bed. And Amy said...

There follows a series of lively escapades: swinging on Gran's curtains, painting Gran's walls green, picking Gran's flowers, making a bike track in Gran's garden, ending up with Amy falling SPLOSH in the mud. The story ends on a happy note.

> Gran never gets cross!
> She put us both in the bath and
> the water was lovely and warm.

Martin Waddell is an artist with a keen ear for the spoken word and his use of language is unparalleled. This story is guaranteed to make young children become completely absorbed and chuckle with delight.

> A story that makes us laugh without malice is to be treasured...Comic writing both reflects and experiments with the familiar world and represents our reality; and comedy for children tends to be most effective when it is robust, springing from characters whose actions upset and embarrass convention and power. Children laugh most readily at comic writing which evokes a picture and sound, bringing antics and collisions alive in the theatre of the imagination.
>
> (Jones and Buttrey 1970)

2. The Great Sharp Scissors *by Philippa Pearce, from* Lion at School and Other Stories, *Puffin (Years 2 and 3).*

The Great Sharp Scissors by Philippa Pearce contains a fast-moving plot, rounded characters, a spareness in the prose and sharp, clear dialogue. The twelve page story is full of wit, wisdom and suspense and will captivate a young audience. It begins:

> Once there was a boy called Tim who was often naughty. Then his mother used to say, 'Tim!' and his father shouted, 'Tim!' But his granny said, 'Tim's a good boy, really.'

The reader's interest is immediately aroused. Tim resents being left alone while his mother visits his poorly Granny.

> He scowled and stamped his foot. He was very angry.

Tim's mother warns him not to let anyone into the house but when a strange man calls and offers to sell him a most remarkable pair of great sharp scissors which will cut anything, Tim cannot resist:

> 'I'll have them,' said Tim.

With the great sharp scissors in his hand, he now has the opportunity to give vent to his feelings. He snip snaps the buttons off his father's coat, he cuts the carpet into hundreds of little pieces, he chops the legs off the tables and chairs and the clashing blades slice though the clock on the mantelpiece.

By now Tim knew that the great sharp scissors would cut anything. They would cut through all the wooden doors and floors. They would cut through all the bricks of all the walls, until nothing was left. Nothing. Tim went and sat at the bottom step of the stairs and cried.

Fortunately, his second visitor, a strange woman who smiles kindly at him, exchanges the scissors for some special magic glue. When Tim's mother arrives back from Granny's, Tim has repaired everything and the house is back to normal. The story ends on the ironic but immensely warm and reassuring note which is never missed by the little listeners.

'Granny's much better, and sends her love. I see you've been a good boy, Tim. Everything neat and tidy …' She made a pot of tea, and she and Tim had tea and bread and butter and raspberry jam. In the middle of it, Tim's father came home, and he had some of the raspberry jam too.

3. The Marble Crusher *by Michael Morpurgo, Mammoth, illustrated by Linda Birch (Years 3 and 4)*

There is real sincerity in Michael Morpurgo's writing. His plots are both exciting and thought-provoking and combine humour with a deep understanding of children's thoughts and feelings. Albert is ten years old, 'a quiet, gentle sort of boy with a thatch of stiff hair that he twiddled when he was nervous'. And Albert gets really, really nervous when he starts his new school, a 'school which was noisy and full of strange faces.' He is teased because the gentle, smiling, good-natured boy is easy to tease and he believes anything people tell him.

'My dad,' said Sid Creedy, 'he played Centre Forward for Liverpool. Did for years. Then they asked him to play for England, but he didn't want to – he didn't like the colour of the shirt.'

Albert believes all the tall stories Sid tells him – that the balding Mr. Cooper is not a teacher at all but 'an escaped monk', that Mr. Manners has 6 wives like Henry the Eighth and 22 children and that the head teacher has a monstrous marble-crushing machine. There is the gripping scene when Albert is discovered playing marbles, a game which has been banned in school.

He was crouching under the teacher's table, taking careful aim, when Mr. Manners came in behind him silently.
'Albert,' he said. 'Albert, are you playing marbles?'
'Oh … Yes sir,' and Albert remembered at once – he remembered the punishment too and began to twiddle his hair.
'They will have to go, all of them mind,' said Mr. Manners. 'Empty your pockets, lad,' and he held out his big chalky hand. 'I'm surprised at you, Albert, and disappointed – very disappointed.'

There is no sentimentality or condescension in this story; it is full of gusto, lively authentic dialogue, immediacy and wit.

In the Literacy Hour (Shared Reading at Key Stage 2) it is suggested that the teacher demonstrates reading strategies using a shared text, focusing on the writer's intention. There is a high level of interaction in this activity, where pupils are encouraged to respond to the teacher's questions through offering suggestions, referring to the text to support personal opinions, linking with their own personal experiences, examining how a text is constructed and exploring the features of the language used. *The Marble Crusher* is a short story ideal for a study of narrative structure, setting, character, use of dialogue, significant detail and the effective use of language.

4. **Hurricane Summer** *by Robert Swindells, Mammoth (Years 5 and 6)*

Robert Swindells's skill as a storyteller is second to none. His novels and short stories, which frequently deal with issues fundamental to children growing up and learning how to cope, are invariably funny, sad, exciting and totally compelling. *Hurricane Summer*, set at the time of the Second World War, has a challenging and fast-moving plot centring on Jim, who worships the brave, dashing, daredevil fighter pilot, Cocky, who lodges at his house. Words are used sparingly but to great effect, characterisation is strong and Swindells weaves a gripping story guaranteed to captivate older juniors. The opening of the novel immediately hooks the reader:

> Funny things friendships. They tend to come and go, but most people have a special friend who stands out among all the others. I'm lucky. I've got two. One of them's been dead a long time now, but it doesn't matter – he'll always be my friend. As for the other...well as I said, friendships are funny. Best thing I can do is tell you about them.

Jim is bullied at school by Clive Simcox, a large, unpleasant, lonely boy who ambushes his victim on the way from school. Jim is really frightened of Simcox and tries to keep out of his way but with little success.

> He used to wait for me in the mornings too, and trip me as I ran past. I'd arrive at school with grazed knees and dirt on my blazer and red eyes from crying and everybody would know Clive had had another go at me.

What makes Jim feel worse is that he is constantly reminded of his cowardice when he sees Cocky, the fearless fighter pilot with the infectious grin – 'a big gangly schoolboy for whom the War was nothing but a rippling adventure.' Then one day Jim learns the truth, the truth that Cocky lives in constant fear.

> He turned his head to look at me. 'And you think we're fearless Jim? You think I'm not afraid?' He snorted. 'I'll tell you this Jim. If I could – if I dared – I'd get up right now and start running, and I wouldn't stop till I was somewhere they'd never find me. And that's true of all fighter pilots.'

The novel moves to an exciting and poignant climax where Jim, knowing that he is not the only one in the world to feel frightened and lonely, faces the bully.

Hurricane Summer is an ideal text for reading aloud and for discussing themes and motives. It can be used successfully for 'guided reading' as part of the Literacy Hour. Children could explore the author's point of view, identify and discuss explicit and implicit meanings, analyse characters and examine the language and structure.

Amy Said, The Great Sharp Scissors, The Marble Crusher and *Hurricane Summer* have all the qualities which are important when thinking about the books to present to young people. The powerful and carefully-crafted language has an immediate appeal. Children enjoy reading and hearing about those very much like themselves. They love tales about boys and girls like Amy and Tim, Albert and Jim, who have moods and get angry as they do, who sometimes feel lonely and afraid, who are sometimes naughty and get into trouble but who, in the end, receive the reassurance of being loved and wanted. They enjoy sharing the experiences and emotions which a well-written story triggers and willingly project into it their own feelings of fear, insecurity anger, joy and relief.

Good writers, like Waddell, Pearce, Morpurgo and Swindells, never patronise their young readers. They know that children are curious, eager, sharply observant and that they love stories that absorb their attention and which make demands upon them. Such stories are important in developing children's language but they are also significant in developing children's emotional literacy. They explore ideas of right and wrong, jealousy, friendship, disappointment, fear and happiness, being accepted and rejected, moral dilemmas and the making of choices, in which the characters ultimately find security, comfort and love. They go to the very heart of children's joys and anxieties.

Chapter 2
The Reading Teacher

Before recommending a range of other good quality books, I need to state the obvious: teachers must be reading teachers if they hope to promote the reading of the children they teach. They need to enthuse about books, recommend titles and authors, read extracts to whet the appetite, regularly ask children about what they are reading and have enjoyed and let children see that they themselves gain great satisfaction and pleasure from reading. Research has revealed again and again that the teacher's impact on children's book choices and on their language development is considerable. The two most important factors in fostering children's reading are teacher influence and the provision of a wide range of material. So, teachers must be readers themselves. There is no short cut, no easy answer, no definitive booklist. Teachers need to have read the books they present to children, they need to select them with care and knowledge and be skilled in judging when and how to use them. Keeping up with the plethora of material is time-consuming and demanding but it is also highly enjoyable and rewarding.

Teachers might keep up with their reading in a number of ways:

1. By having close and regular contact with The Schools Library Service. The librarians advise on and recommend titles, organise courses and conferences, workshops and book reviewing groups and produce fiction, poetry and non-fiction lists. Teachers might try to visit The School Library Service HQ on a regular basis and depart with a small collection of books for reading: a couple of picture books, a poetry collection, a short story anthology, some recently published non-fiction texts, perhaps a controversial children's story about which the librarian wants an opinion and one or two books the librarian feels they might enjoy.
2. By keeping in close and regular contact with a good bookshop. Suppliers who specialise in children's literature like Sonia Benster of The Children's Bookshop, 37–39 Lidget Street, Lindley, Huddersfield HD3 3JF and Madeleine Lindley of the Book Centre, Broadgate, Bradway Business Park, Chadderton, Oldham OL9 9XA, are widely-read and select books with knowledge and care. They will send material, recommend titles, tell their customers what new

publications have come on the market and which are the most popular with children. They will also attend teachers' courses and parents' evenings to mount displays and sell books. The Country Bookstore, Hassop Station, Near Bakewell in Derbyshire (e-mail: mail@countrybookstore.co.uk) is an on-line bookstore with over 15,000 titles in stock and with 1.5 million titles listed. Teachers can search by title, author or key word, browse numerous categories, including author information, and place orders on-line for titles in print not only in the United Kingdom but those published in the United States. The store can also do a search for out-of-print titles.

3. By becoming a member of The Reading and Language Information Centre, based at The University of Reading. Members automatically receive new books every term, have free access to the permanent display of 15,000 children's books and teachers' resources and receive a discount on past publications which include: *Practical Ways to Organise Reading, Fiction in the Literacy Hour, Children Making Books, Individualised Reading, Directory of Authors, Storytelling in Schools, How Schools Teach Reading, Helping Your Child with Reading and Reading IT.* The Centre has an e-mail address (reading-centre@reading.ac.uk) and a website (httpp:/www.rdg.ac.uk/AcaDepts/eh/ReadLang/home.html) for updates and further information.

4. By reading the reviews. Over the school holidays teachers might catch up on the new books reviewed in such journals and booklets as those produced by The Thimble Press and *Child Education*. The bookseller, Waterstones, produces an excellent *Guide to Children's Books*, an annotated booklist in which the very best of classic and contemporary fiction books for children are reviewed. *The Good Book Guide to Children's Books*, published by Penguin Books, is also a must.

5. By becoming a member of The School Library Association, Liden Library, Barrington Close, Liden, Swindon. SN3 6HF. The SLA provides a range of published guidelines and booklists, a quarterly journal, *The School Librarian*, with articles and book reviews and CD-ROMS, local and national training courses, a network of local branches, a help-line for members and an advisory and information service.

6. By visiting one of the national exhibitions. Educational Exhibitions Ltd, 14 Gainsborough Road, London. N12 8AG, organise a comprehensive range of exhibitions which take place throughout the country and which include the North of England Conference and Exhibition, the BETT Show at Olympia, the NATE Annual Conference, the Education Show at the Birmingham NEC, Wales Education Conference and the North West Regional Conference and Exhibition. All the major publishers are represented and teachers can view the recently published books, materials and reading resources.

7. By listening to children and finding out what they enjoy reading. Some writers such as Helen Cresswell, Gene Kemp and Dick King-Smith have a universal appeal, others; like Margaret Mahy, Diana Wynne Jones and William Mayne, are an acquired taste and some, like Ivan Southall, Penelope Lively and Meindert Dejong, they learn to like given time. The stories children enjoy depend on a number of factors: age and maturity, ability, environment, experience and interests, even the mood they are in at a particular time. Like adults, children

have preferences and a story which one child will read avidly might have little impact on another.

Some teachers find it useful to keep a record of what they have read with brief notes about the book for future reference. A simple and easy to complete example is shown below.

STORY RECORD

Title: *The Hodgeheg*

Author: Dick King-Smith

Author Information: Farmer, teacher, freelance writer. Writes original, un-sentimental, entertaining stories which appeal to all children.

Genre: Amusing animal adventure story.

Plot: The hedgehogs at Number 5A dream of reaching the Park. Max sets out to solve the problem of how to get them across the busy main road.

Language: Very accessible, lively, sometimes poetic.

Related Texts: *Ace, Daggie Dogfoot, Dodos are Forever, Emily's Leg, The Fox Busters, Friends and Brothers, George Speaks, Harry's Mad, Magnus Powermouse, Martin's Mice, Noah's Brother, Paddy's Pot of Gold, The Queen's Nose, Saddlebottom, The Sheep-Pig, Sophie's Snail.*

Age Range: 6–10 years.

Chapter 3

Some recommended texts

The National Literacy Framework for Teaching sets out clearly the teaching objectives for Reception to Year 6 and outlines the kinds of stories, poems, plays and non-fiction texts children should encounter as they progress through the primary years. Central to the Framework is the Literacy Hour, a dedicated time each day where the teacher develops children's reading skills through instruction, questioning, eliciting responses and refining and extending children's contributions. The Literacy Hour is not, however, about going through a minimum of texts in maximum, pleasure-destroying detail, interrogating the writing in such a way that children are turned off books and reading. As David Blunkett states: 'The Literacy Hour enables children to learn poetry, prose and creative writing, with access to more texts than ever before.' (*The Times*, Friday 23 July 1999). It is about developing in children a love of reading by using a wide range of really interesting and challenging books and dealing with these books in a sensitive way. This material should include the elements listed overleaf.

PROSE

Nursery Tales	Folk Tales	Traditional Stories
Wonder Tales	Fairy Tales	Stories with Familiar Settings
Tall Stories	Anecdotes	Family History Stories
Jokes	Tongue-Twisters	Puns
Word Puzzles	Warning Tales	Fables
Myths	Legends	Sagas
Parables	Dilemma Stories	Stories from Different Cultures
School Stories	Historical Stories	Science Fiction
Ghost Stories	Mystery Stories	Humorous Stories
Fantasy Stories	Monologues	Adventure Stories

POETRY

Playground Chants	Nursery Rhymes	Miniature Poems
Simple Counting Rhymes	Action Verse	Syllabic Poetry
Songs and Lyrics	Rhythmic Verse	Haiku
Rhyming Couplets	Clerihews	Tanka
Patterned Poems	Kennings	Cinquains
Humorous Verse	Free Verse	Performance Poetry
Tongue-Twisters	Prayers	Conversation Poems
Alphabet Poems	Riddles	Narrative Poetry
Limericks	Shape/Concrete Poems	Ballads
Choral Verse	Acrostics	Epitaphs

NON-FICTION

Simple Non-Fiction Texts	Simple Instructions	Information Texts
Signs	Simple Dictionaries	Glossaries
Labels	Retelling of Events	Indexes
Captions	Recounts of Visits	Thesauruses
Lists	Non-Chronological Reports	Explanations
Letters	Encyclopaedias	Articles
Newspapers	Magazines	Advertisements
Circulars	Flyers	Discussion Texts
Debates	Editorials	Leaflets
Rules	Recipes	Directions
Commentaries	Diaries	Journals
Biography	Autobiography	Anecdotes
Reference Texts	Discussion Texts	Public Documents

Through the range of texts described on the following pages, teachers are offered suggestions for stories and poems to use in the Literacy Hour, which reflect the recommendations contained in the Literacy Strategy. It also satisfies the National Curriculum requirements for wide reading. The list is very selective and contains only a small number of the 90,000 or so children's books in print. Last year over

7,000 new titles were published. The books recommended are those which many children have read and enjoyed, which fulfil the criteria outlined earlier in this chapter, and in some measure represent the great variety of reading material now available. The selection is not necessarily the best and I guess that some readers will feel many well-tried favourites and much loved books have been omitted. The books suggested will appeal to children, and offer excellent opportunities for word, sentence and text-level work. The stories, poems and non-fiction material can be used for 'shared' and for 'guided' reading and also for independent reading outside the Literacy Hour.

Ten picture books

> The greatest teachers of reading and writing in Britain today are David McKee, Shirley Hughes, Anthony Browne, Graham Oakley, John Burningham, the Ahlbergs, Jan Pienkowski and a host of others like them. Their intensive courses are very modestly priced and come 'packaged' in the form of wonderful picture books.
>
> (Hynds in Waterland, 1988)

There is now a vast range of picture books, varied in design, story and illustration. Good picture books, like the ones described below, foster the skills of reading, stimulating and supporting the early reader as she or he struggles to decode print. They also have a great emotional impact. The picture books of John Burningham and Shirley Hughes, for instance, with their themes of mums and dads, friends, neighbours, gardens, shopping, pets, babies and everyday family life have a massive appeal. They are warm, funny, entertaining, reassuring books and children recognise the situations and identify with the wonderfully rounded characters who, like real children, get angry, fearful and frustrated and who are sometimes naughty.

1. Alfie Gets in First *by Shirley Hughes, Bodley Head*

All Shirley Hughes' books are heart-warming, appealing, cleverly written and illustrated with witty panache. Children deserve to hear them read aloud and have access to them on the library shelves. In this good-natured story, Alfie locks his mum and the baby outside with amusing results. In *The Snow Lady* (6–9 year olds), Samantha, Sam for short, loves playing in the street with her dog and her friend Barney but her next-door neighbour, Mrs. Mean, is always complaining. Other books by Shirley Hughes include: *Another Helping of Chips* (6–9 year olds), *Chips and Jessie* (6–9 year olds), *Here Comes Charlie Moon* (6–9 year olds), *Hiding* (6–9 year olds), and *It's Too Frightening for Me* (7–9 year olds). *Dogger* (3–8 year olds) is another delightful portrait of a minor family crisis when Dave loses his favourite toy.

2. Whatever Next! *by Jill Murphy, Macmillan*

'Can I go to the moon?' asked Baby Bear.
'No you can't,' said Mrs. Bear. 'It's bathtime.'

Whatever Next! is a cleverly-written and captivating story with lively, colourful and humorously-detailed illustrations. Other splendid stories by Jill Murphy include: *The Worst Witch* (7–9 year olds), *A Bad Spell for the Worst Witch* (7–9 year olds) and *The Worst Witch Strikes Again* (7–9 year olds). Her novel *Worlds Apart*, suitable for older readers (11 year olds), is a poignant account about a young girl growing up, knowing nothing about her father who left home when she was a baby. When she is 11 Susan learns about her father and determines to find him.

3. Monsters *by Russell Hoban, Gollancz*

Monsters! Monsters! Monsters! John just cannot stop drawing them. His obsession leads to strange and disturbing events! *Bread and Jam for Frances, Bedtime for Frances* and *Best Friends for Frances*, by the same author, with pencil drawings by Lillian Hoban, are three other captivating and sympathetic tales for younger readers. Hoban's novel, *A Mouse and his Child*, and suitable for 10 and 11 year olds, is an exciting and poignant adventure story about the clockwork mice who search for their lost home.

4. Willy the Wimp *by Anthony Browne, Magnet*

Poor, lonely Willy is frightened of everybody. When the suburban gorilla gang picks on him and call him Willy the Wimp, he decides that enough is enough and action is called for. Exercises, special diet, aerobics, boxing and body-building, transform Willy into a force to be reckoned with. This is a delightfully sharp, sophisticated and amusing story. The sequel, *Willy the Champ*, (6–9 year olds), is equally entertaining. *Piggybook*, (6–11 year olds), by the same author, is a delightfully inventive book about stereotyping, described in *The Good Book Guide* as 'a superb and unforgettably funny picture book about male chauvinist piggery.' The overworked, undervalued Mrs. Piggott, who waits hand and foot on her boorish husband and two lazy sons, finally ups and leaves them to their own devices. All the things in the house – wallpaper, doorknobs, even the father and sons themselves – undergo some curious changes. In the simply told and superbly illustrated story, *Changes*, the effect a new baby has on an older child is explored sensitively and with great warmth. 'That morning his father had gone to fetch Joseph's mother. Before leaving, he'd said that things were going to change.' Joseph doesn't know what his father meant.

5. Each Peach Pear Plum *by Janet and Allan Ahlberg, Picture Puffin*

A delightfully simple and fascinating collection of rhyming couplets featuring familiar nursery rhyme characters like Cinderella, Baby Bunting, the Three Bears and Mother Hubbard who are all hiding craftily in the pictures. Allan Ahlberg's writing is highly original and full of humour and has an enormous appeal to children and adults. His other books are well worth adding to your collection: *The Clothes Horse*, stories which can be read to younger children but are equally entertaining for older ones; *Happy Families*, (4–7 year olds), a collection full of repetition and rhythm, which makes it ideal for using with children mastering reading; *The Jolly Postman*, (3–11 year olds), a highly original and interactive book, splendid for sharing and exploring; *Burglar Bill*, (5–8 year olds), about the loveable character who reforms when he meets the delightful Burglar Betty; *Jeremiah in the Dark Woods*, (7–9 years olds), a captivating, superbly-illustrated account based on traditional stories; *Ten in a Bed*, (8–10 year olds), a collection of witty parodies of well known fairy tales; *Woof*, (9–11 year olds) about Eric who changes into the chocolate loving, cat-hating dog and which was made into a popular television series.

6. Connie Came to Play *by Jill Paton Walsh, Puffin Books*

When Connie visits Robert's house to play, Robert is grumpy and won't let her touch any of his toys. 'Everything's mine,' he says. 'All right,' replies Connie, 'I'll play in my head.' With wonderfully bright and humorous illustrations, this gently perceptive and linguistically rich story explores how kind little Connie deals with the selfish boy who won't let her play with his toys. Jill Paton Walsh is a writer of exceptional skill and her other books are essential additions to the classroom library: the poetic *Babylon* (6–8 year olds), the spooky *Birdy and The Ghostie* (7–9 year olds) and the wonderfully descriptive *The Butty Boy* (8–11 year olds).

7. Six Dinner Sid *by Inga Moore, Simon and Schuster*

Sid, the crafty cat, lives in six houses and eats six dinners each day, unbeknown to his six owners. Each night he slips out of number one and moves from house to house eating a delicious variety of meals. Life is wonderful for this clever cat until he is found out. 'One cold damp day, he caught a nasty cough.' The next thing he knows poor Sid is off to the vet – not once but six times! This is an affectionate and witty tale with a lively plot and detailed illustrations.

8. The Very Lonely Firefly *by Eric Carle, Hamish Hamilton*

Fireflies are not flies but little beetles that wink and blink in the night to attract other fireflies. This beautifully written story is about one very lonely little firefly and his search for his friends. There is a sparkling surprise on the last page. Another of Eric Carle's captivating stories is about *The Very Hungry Caterpillar* (4–8 year olds) who eats his way through the pages of the book.

9. A Present for Paul *by Bernard Ashley, Collins Picture Lions*

It is Saturday and baby Paul is teething. Dad takes Pleasure to the market shopping where she hopes to buy her little brother a present. But the market is big, crowded and noisy and Pleasure gets lost. All of Bernard Ashley's superb stories are concerned with children growing up and learning to cope with family, friends and school. This is a touching account, evocatively illustrated, about the warm, happy relationship between a father and his little daughter. Other Bernard Ashley stories, with clear plots, lively dialogue, well drawn characters and plenty of humour, include: *Dinner Ladies Don't Count* (7–9 year olds), *I'm Trying to Tell You* (7–9 year olds), *Your Guess is as Good as Mine* (7–9 year olds) and *A Bit of Give and Take* (7–9 year olds). His novels for older readers, *All My Men*, *Break in the Sun*, *The Trouble with Donovan Croft*, all with riveting plots, superb character portrayal and often set firmly in a harsh world, rank as some of the best children's novels ever written.

10. Fred *by Posy Simmonds, Jonathan Cape*

This warm, funny story, with beautifully vivid illustrations, is an effective blend of comic strip and picture book. When Sophie and Bick's cat dies they discover that the sly creature has been leading an outrageous double life as a rock star. *Lulu and the Flying Babies* and *The Chocolate Wedding*, also by Posy Simmonds, are richly-illustrated and equally memorable.

Some more picture book recommendations

- *Old MacDonald had a Farm* (ISBN 1 55858 281 9) (traditional rhyme);
- *The Willow Pattern Story* by Allan Drummond (ISBN 1 55858 171 5) (story from another culture);
- *Arthur* by Amanda Graham and Donna Gynell (ISBN 0 947212 12 4) (story with familiar setting);
- *The Nightingale* by Hans Christian Andersen (ISBN 0 90723 457 7) (traditional fairy story);
- *The Rainbow Fish* by Marcus Pfister (ISBN 1 55858 441 2) (story with predictable structure);
- *Imagine* by Alison Lester (ISBN 1 86373 262 4) (fantasy story);
- *The Owl and the Pussycat* by Edward Lear (ISBN 1 55858 467 6) (poem by significant children's poet);
- *The Children of Lir* by Sheila MacGill-Callahan (ISBN 1 85714 128 8) (historical picture book);
- *Why?* by Nikolai Popov (ISBN 1 55858 996 1) (story which deals with an issue);
- *Survival* by Guundie Kuchling (ISBN 1 86374 274 3) (early information text);
- *A Gallery of Children* by A.A. Milne (ISBN 0 85692 179 3) (story by significant children's author);
- *Fabulous Places of Myth* by Robert Inkpen (ISBN 0 85091 839 1) (myth);
- *The Hare and the Tortoise* (ISBN 1 84011 0888885 6) (fable);
- *You Can Do Great Lettering* by Kim Gamble (ISBN 1 86373 864 9) (instruction book);
- *How the Body Works*, a Moonlight First Dictionary (ISBN 1 85103 252 5) (non-fiction book/first dictionary).

Ten novelty and pop-up books

> Pop-up books have never been more popular but they are often frowned upon, and with reason, by reading experts. Unless carefully-chosen, they offer a play experience rather than a reading one.
>
> (Landsberg 1990)

Despite the frowning experts, children are delighted and fascinated by many pop-up books; they love the cleverness and originality and enjoy the element of surprise. The worst kind of pop-up books are mass-produced and fall apart after just a few readings.

The prose is mechanical and the illustrations garish. The very best pop-up books are sturdy with well-written texts – they are masterpieces of paper engineering, designed to stimulate and support the beginning reader through lively narrative, lyrical repetition of language, verbal jokes and bright, original illustrations. The most comprehensive and unusual selection of pop-up books, die-cut reading books, flap books and novelty books with puppets, squeakers and moving parts, is produced by Child's Play International. The early reader is encouraged to touch, listen, watch, act out, sing, join in, as well as read the lively text. Children who do not, as yet, have the necessary reading skills, are encouraged to communicate through the spoken word and through rhyme and rhythms, to experience the language. The range includes:

1. Phone Book *by Jan Pienkowski, Orchard Books*

Push the little red button on the front and the telephone will ring, but the whole menagerie of pop-up animals are just too busy to answer it. Jan Pienkowski has written and constructed dozens of delightfully inventive and beautifully finished pop-up books. *Dinnertime, Gossip, Toilet Book* ('don't forget to flush it!'), *Little Monsters* and *Small Talk* (4–6 year olds) are but a few. *Haunted House* (5–8 year olds) has monsters, ghosts, ghouls and things that go bump in the night and which jump from the page. In *Fancy That* (4–6 year olds), the story of the old woman who swallowed the fly is here in pop-up form.

2. Maisy Goes to Bed *by Lucy Cousins, Walker Books*

Maisy Goes to Bed and *Maisy Goes to Playschool* are warm, original and interactive stories for very young children with bold, bright pictures and sturdy construction. Little fingers love to pull tabs and lift flaps as they help Maisy, the little mouse, to get ready for bed.

3. Ruth's Loose Tooth *by Nicholas A. Kerna, Child's Play International*

Ruth is a great brown cow with an old wiggly tooth. Everyone tries to help her pull it out. The mouse and the goat, the fish and the crow and a variety of other helpful animals and birds tug and toil through the text, each of them heaving on a long piece of string which stretches from page to page. This clever little book is part of the *Child's Play Action Books* Series. Others include *Curious Kittens, The Peek-o-Boo Riddle Book* and *Hide and Seek* (4–7 year olds).

4. Missing Dad *by Carla Dijs, Child's Play International*

'Help I'm lost, I want my dad!' cries the tiger cub, raising a sad little head. He asks the great lumbering polar bear, the ostrich which lifts an enormous neck, the crocodile which snaps long green jaws and rattles a set of sharp teeth, until at long last he finds his missing dad. 'Dad am I glad to see you!' he squeals in delight. 'There is no-one like you in the whole wide world.' A deceptively simple and appealing story guaranteed to bring a smile to the lips and a lump to the throat. *Missing Mum* (4–7 year olds) is in the same series.

5. A Cheese and Tomato Spider *by Nick Sharratt, Andre Deutsch*

A big, bright, boldly illustrated pick 'n' mix book where children can jumble up characters and creatures in a wonderfully bizarre text. Ever met a strawberry-flavoured granny or an exploding man or a deep-sea lemon or a wriggly cake? You will in this crazy, mixed-up world. Other ingenious books by Nick Sharratt include: *Don't Put Your Finger in the Jelly, Nelly!*, *Ketchup on Your Cornflakes?* and *Zoopermarket* (5–8 years olds).

6. What's in the Cave? *by Peter Seymour, Child's Play International*

A witty pop-up book where children are encouraged to find out what is lurking in the cave by lifting a series of flaps. There is a lazy lizard, a fat bat, a sneaky snake, a friendly frog, a sly spider, a broody bird, a busy beetle and finally the wonderfully coloured and captivating monster which will make all the little ones gasp in surprise.

7. The Most Amazing Hide and Seek Alphabet Book *by Robert Crowther, Viking*

A fascinating and interactive journey through the alphabet. Children will enjoy searching for the details in the pictures.

8. Ladybird Moves Home *by Richard Fowler, Transworld*

An ingeniously simple story in which the little ladybird plods her way through the world of words. Children will enjoy joining in.

9. Patrick and the Puppy *by Peter Seymour, Child's Play International*

A delightful finger puppet book. The little reader has to help Patrick find the puppy something good to eat. The little finger puppet wags, nods and shakes his head through the captivating text.

10. No Matter What *by Arnold Shapiro, Child's Play International*

Big or small, short or tall, fat or thin, out or in . . . No matter who we are or how we look or what we do, there is always someone who loves us. This gentle book should be essential reading for all children – and adults.

Some more novelty and pop-up book recommendations

- *Splashtime Giants* (ISBN 0 85953 329 8) (bath book);
- *I don't want to have a bath!* (ISBN 1 85430 616 2) (board book);
- *Santa's Busy Day!* (ISBN 1 85430 605 7) (lift-the-flap book);
- *Nine Naughty Kittens* (ISBN 1 85430 625 1) (split-page novelty book);
- *Noah's Ark* (ISBN 0 85953 255 0) (three-dimensional, pull-out book);
- *The Helpful Shoelace* (ISBN 0 85953 287 6) (novelty book with real shoelace);

- *There were ten in a bed* (ISBN 0 85953 095 7) (interactive sing-and-count book with turning dial);
- *Amazing Senses* (ISBN 0 85953 284 4) (interactive tactile novelty book with activities, experiments, blind spots and reflexes);
- *Dinosaurs* (ISBN 0 85953 546 0) (non-fiction pop-up book);
- *Counting Kids* (ISBN 0 85953 241 0) (bead-frame activity book).

Ten folk and fairy tale collections

> There are some stories that no child should miss: fairy tales, legends and myths. Fairy stories are genuine children's literature, and we know that there are deep and abiding links between the childhood of mankind as preserved in these stories and the early life of each of us.
>
> (Meek 1982)

The familiarity of the fairy tale and the folk tale, the magic and fantasy, the wild, wonderful and exaggerated characters, the fast action and terrible events, the constant repetitions and finally the happy ending where good triumphs over evil, all combine to create a powerful and fascinating story which captures the child's imagination and remains with him or her long after it has been heard. Characters like Cinderella, Rapunzel, Red Riding Hood, Jack and the Beanstalk and Snow White will appear in different guises throughout fairy tale literature. The stories are sometimes about kings and castles, brave princes and archetypal evil witches, giants and trolls, wicked stepmothers and fairy godmothers, but can also be about ordinary people, their hopes, dreams, shrewdness and heroism. There are many traditional and modern folk and fairy tale anthologies, and teachers need to explore collections from all over the world which offer insights into other cultures and into other times. Here are just a few:

1. **Classic Fairy Tales,** *Puffin*

There is a wealth of English, Irish, Scottish and Welsh folk and fairy tales in this attractive volume, some well-known, others less familiar, but all rattling good reads.

2. **British and Irish Folk Tales** *by Kevin Crossley-Holland,* *Orchard Books*

This splendid collection contains the most popular of traditional stories, all told in clear, accessible language and with great verve and lively description. Kevin Crossley-Holland has produced many volumes of fairy and folk tales including: *The Dead Moon and Other Tales from East Anglia and the Fen Country* (9–11 year olds) and *The Faber Book of Northern Folk Tales* (9–11 year olds).

3. **Bag of Moonshine** *by Alan Garner, Collins*

A delightful, well-illustrated collection packed with classic stories containing all the dramatic elements of the folk tale: envy, greed, love, tragedy and the search for happiness. Alan Garner is a master storyteller who brings the tales to life superbly.

4. Stories from Hans Andersen *by Andrew Matthews, Orchard Books*

Carefully illustrated by Alan Snow, this lively and accessible collection contains all of Hans Christian Andersen's well-loved tales, including *The Ugly Duckling*, *The Little Match Girl* and *Thumbelina*.

5. Three Indian Princesses: The Stories of Savitri, Damayanti and Sita *by Jamila Gavin, Methuen*

This richly detailed and carefully-crafted collection of Indian folk tales is ideal for encouraging children to discuss and explore some of the underlying themes of the folk tale: goodness, generosity, honesty, truth and the triumph of the weak and vulnerable over the strong and powerful. Also worth reading is Jamila Gavin's collection of traditional Hindu stories, *The Hindu World* (9–11 year olds).

6. Anancy – Spiderman *by James Berry, Walker Books*

Anancy, the clever and mischievous Spiderman, outwits everybody. This collection of Caribbean folk tales provides an excellent resource for reading aloud and for further study. Children will listen attentively and join in with the lively rhythmic language.

7. Listen to This Story: Tales from The West Indies *by Grace Hallworth, Methuen*

This is an anthology of wonderfully atmospheric tales with pace, suspense and lively language. It is full of resourceful and imaginative characters and vigorous plots. This is a collection the reader just cannot put down. Also by Grace Hallworth is *A Web of Stories* (8–11 year olds).

8. The People Could Fly: American Black Folk Tales *by Virginia Hamilton, Walker Books*

There is a whole range of human emotions in these wonderfully detailed and rhythmic tales. Carefully structured, richly illustrated and with humour and suspense, these stories are totally compelling.

9. Book of Creation Stories *by Margaret Mayo, Orchard*

In every culture there is an explanation of how the world began – the story of creation. In this fascinating and magical collection, Margaret Mayo retells ten stories from around the world in a lively and direct way.

10. The Faber Book of Favourite Fairy Tales *by Sara and Stephen Corrin, Faber and Faber*

Sara and Stephen Corrin have spent a lifetime collecting the most entertaining and unusual folk and fairy tales. Over the years they have compiled a whole range of modern and traditional story collections intended for particular age groups: *Stories for the Under Fives, Stories for Six Year Olds and Other Young Readers, Stories for Seven Year Olds* and so on. Each collection is based on a theme, for example there are heroes and heroines for the eight year olds and humour for the nine year olds.

Some more folk and fairy tale recommendations

* *Kofi and the Butterflies* (ISBN 1 870516 16 31 1);
* *Dave and the Tooth Fairy* (ISBN 1 870516 13 3);
* *The Sleeping Beauty* (ISBN 0 7500 2001 6);
* *Little Red Riding Hood* (ISBN 0 7500 2003 2);
* *Stories from the Amazon* (ISBN 0 7502 2423 1);
* *West African Twister Tales* (ISBN 0 19 274172 1;
* *Native American Tales* (ISBN 07502 2271 9);
* *African Tales* (ISBN 0 7502 2272 7);
* *West Indian Folk Tales* (ISBN 0 19 274127 6);
* *The Oxford Treasury of World Stories* (ISBN 0 19 278144 8);
* *The Oxford Treasury of Children's Stories* (ISBN 0 19 278156 1).

Ten big books

Reading is much more than the decoding of black and white marks upon a page; it is a quest for meaning and one which requires the reader to be an active participant. It is the prerequisite of successful teaching of reading, especially in the early stages, that whenever techniques are taught or books chosen for children's use, meaning should always be in the foreground.

(DES 1988b)

The use of 'big books' or enlarged texts is a feature of the Literacy Strategy. Sharing stories, poems and non-fiction material with the whole group in the first part of the Literacy Hour, the teacher actively involves the children with the text, demonstrating how the 'black and white marks upon a page' carry meaning. She may work from the same big book over five days with a combination of reading and linked writing activities. In this period children will be encouraged to listen attentively, think about the story or poem, talk about the situations and the characters, join in the reading, offer their views, interpret the pictures, anticipate and predict, point out significant words and phrases, use their knowledge of context and sentence structure in their 'quest for meaning'. There is a plethora of big books for both Key Stages on the market but the ones listed below have been tried and tested.

1. The Big Hungry Bear *by Don and Audrey Wood,* *Child's Play International*

There is only one way in the whole, wide world to save the ripe, red strawberry from the big hungry Bear...This bright, beautifully illustrated book has an immediate appeal and children will be intrigued and excited by the simple, entertaining story. They will enjoy talking over the reading and using the various clues to guess the outcome. There is a bright red story sack containing the mouse, strawberry and wooden knife to use alongside the reading and discussing and a *Little Mouse Sequence Game*, where children are encouraged to match words and pictures and undertake a whole range of simple language-based tasks. An audiotape version of the story, read by Patrick Macnee and enriched by music and a catchy song, is also available.

2. Kangaroos *by Martin Waddell, Ginn*

Kate sees a small kangaroo on a trip to the zoo. 'I want one too!' she cries. This pattern and rhyme book has an original story, lots of humour, clever language and plenty of brightly coloured cartoon drawings. The book is ideal for reading with younger and older infants. Pupils might be asked to identify and describe the characters and animals, retell the story, discuss the elements of humorous writing, predict what might happen and draw parts of the story they enjoyed the most.

3. Mrs Honey's Hat, *written and illustrated by Pam Adams,* *Child's Play International*

When Mrs Honey wears her hat little does she know that it will be transformed by a whole menagerie of animals. A delightful text for sharing and exploring, with humorous illustrations and big, bold, well-spaced type, this lively story is ideal for use in the Literacy Hour with very early readers. Children will be able to join in the reading when they feel confident enough, make predictions about what might happen next to Mrs Honey's hat, participate in discussion about the main points of the narrative, retell the story in correct sequence and represent the story in drawings, storyboards, collages and murals. Child's Play International has produced a doll to accompany the story and twelve Velcro hat decorations to attach to Mrs

Honey's hat. The teacher shares out the hat pieces, tells the story and the children pass the doll along adding the various items.

4. My Cat Likes to Hide in Boxes *by Eve Sutton, Puffin*

A wonderfully inventive comic poem with a vibrant rhythm and catchy rhymes and one which speaks to children in a direct, easy way. This is a useful text to teach about the structure of poetry, rhyme, rhythm, alliteration and punctuation. Children might be asked to join in the reading when the poem is reread, supply rhyming words, identify words beginning with the same letter and talk about the new vocabulary which they will encounter.

5. The Royal Dinner *by Brenda Parkes and John Burge, Kingscourt*

The King told the cook, 'I want ham for my dinner, ham for my dinner, or it's OFF WITH YOUR HEAD!' The Queen told the cook, 'I want cheese for my dinner, cheese for my dinner, or it's OFF WITH YOUR HEAD!' Everyone in the palace wants something different. The cook's dilemma is told in a delightfully funny and inventive story full of repetitions and rhymes guaranteed to get the children joining in. This is another text which lends itself to sensitive interrogation.

6. Blast Off! *by Maryann Dobeck, Ginn*

Join the crew of the space shuttle in this simply written and fascinating factual account of a trip into space and back. The photographs are breathtaking and offer ample opportunities for discussion.

7. Children of the Sun *by Arthur John L'Hommedieu, Child's Play International*

The sun is a large star in the centre of our solar system. Nine planets including the Earth orbit around it. Open this book, pull the pages towards you and you enter a tunnel in space visiting the planets in order of their distance from the sun. This amazing, ingenious factual book is a masterpiece of paper engineering and will fascinate children of all ages. It is also available in a smaller format.

8. The Hunter *by Paul Geraghty, Red Fox*

This delightful story is about Jamina, the little girl who sets off one morning to collect honey from the honey bird, only to find herself lost in the African Bush. Frightened and alone, Jamina comes upon a baby elephant whimpering for its mother, killed by poachers. The little creature follows the girl as she searches for home. The story has a clear and predictable structure with a gripping opening, lively language, interesting events, tension and splendid detail. The illustrations are outstanding and capture superbly the vast beauty and wonderful colours of the African landscape.

9. Dinosaur Roar! *by Paul and Henrietta Stickland, Puffin*

This is a brilliant read and will delight, intrigue and amuse young children. The simple, repetitive text engages the reader immediately and is ideal for reading to the whole class without interruption, rereading with the children using different voices and intonations and for encouraging lively talk. The teacher might start by talking about the wonderful pictures on the cover and asking the children to predict what the text is about before sharing the story.

10. A World War Two Anthology *selected by Wendy Body, Pelican Big Books*

For use with older primary children, this intriguing collection of words written both at the time of war and later, cleverly juxtaposes fiction and fact, drawings and photographs. There is a whole range of different forms of writing: poems, accounts, journal extracts, skipping rhymes, pieces of dialogue, extracts from novels, telegrams and letters. The selection contains a superbly poignant and optimistic poem by Richard Eburne, aged 12. It is a very useful resource for use when studying longer texts which take place at the time of the Second World War, novels such as *Carrie's War* (Nina Bawden), *Goodnight Mr. Tom* (Michelle Magorian), *Hurricane Summer* (Robert Swindells), *Conrad's War* (Andrew Davies) and *Dolphin Crossing* (Jill Paton Walsh).

Some more big book recommendations:

- *My Alphabet Big Book* (ISBN 0 19 910636 3);
- *Big Nursery Rhyme Book* (ISBN 0 19 915596 8);
- *What If?* (ISBN 1 885430 498 4);
- *Elmer* (ISBN 0 09926528 1);
- *Willy and Hugh* (ISBN 0 09926615 6);
- *All Join In* (ISBN 009926529 X);
- *Pass the Jam* (ISBN 0 09926614 8);
- *Titch* (ISBN 0 09926613 X);
- *Don't Do That!* (ISBN 0 099266172);
- *Lazy Ozzie* (ISBN 1 85430 603 0);
- *Ridiculous!* (ISBN 1 885430 604 9);
- *Mapwork 1* (ISBN 0 7502 2336 7);
- *History from Photographs* (ISBN 0 7502 2388 X).

Ten story books for younger readers

Books that celebrate the range of life's possibilities, books that acknowledge and delight in the variety of human experience, books that by their virtuosity of language make the reader share in that curiosity and excitement – these are the books that enhance children's lives, that give them food for thought, pique their imaginations and sensibilities and arouse their senses of wonder.

(Landsberg 1990)

The range of story books is vast: fantasy, ghosts, science fiction and animal stories, adventure, mystery, family and school stories, cartoons, nature, evolution, hobbies, sport, history – the list is endless. As teachers, it is our responsibility to bring children and books together and give them a range worth their time and attention. The following small selection might be the core of a classroom library for early readers:

1. Lion at School and Other Stories *by Philippa Pearce, Puffin*

A rich and varied collection of nine funny stories in which the author marries fantasy, magic and everyday reality. This collection contains *The Great Sharp Scissors*. Philippa Pearce's stories are suitable for the 'guided reading' sessions. They have immediate appeal, clear structure, recognisable characters, are of manageable length and they support and challenge the young reader.

2. It Shouldn't Happen to a Frog and Other Stories *by Catherine Storr, Piccolo*

These warm-hearted and satisfying stories are about Lisa, a modern girl caught up in the traditional fairy tales of *The Frog Prince, The Three Bears, Bluebeard* and *Cinderella*. They give a modern twist to the favourite children's tales and are lively, inventive and great fun to read aloud. They offer excellent models for children to write their own 'alternative' fairy tales and on which to base drama activities.

3. Stories From Around the World, *Federation of Children's Book Groups, Hodder and Stoughton*

Over 21.000 children from all over the world took part in the testing of these stories. The aim of the collection is 'for families and teachers to share these stories with children in the hope that it will bring our love of storytelling to others.' The 15 stories range from the affectionate and humorous to the sad and touching and they are written by such accomplished writers as: Anita Desai, Grace Hallworth, Edna O'Brien, Alf Proysen, Joan Aiken and Virginia Hamilton. This collection is ideal for 'guided reading' sessions, offering excellent opportunities for more able children to deepen and widen their understanding of different texts, develop the skills required to read increasingly demanding material, learn about aspects of short story structure, character, description and dialogue and engage in reading strategies such as predicting, locating, checking, confirming and self-correcting.

4. Stories for Christmas *by Alison Uttley, Faber and Faber*

Twelve splendidly magical stories which capture the atmosphere of the special season. They are written with great emotional honesty and warmth by a fine storyteller.

5. Sophie's Snail *by Dick King-Smith, Walker Books*

Sophie is a very independent four year old and is a real handful. This collection of six original and amusing stories has all the warmth, detail and lively language which characterise this outstanding writer. Dick King-Smith speaks to children on their own terms; he never patronises them but captures their imaginations and demonstrates how rich, flexible and delightful language can be. Schools should have all his books.

6. Scottish Highland Tales *by Iain Crighton-Smith, Ward Lock*

Tall tales about the great mountains and desolate lochs drawn from traditional sources to stimulate young minds and encourage lively discussion. They are magical, dreamy and mysterious and include mighty tales about giants, birds transformed into men, seals changed into women, the brown bear of the green glen and the serpent's stone. The tales are enhanced with delightfully robust line drawings by a variety of talented illustrators.

7. A Necklace of Raindrops and Other Stories *by Joan Aiken, Puffin*

These eight enthralling, ingenious and magical stories are told with economy and poetic intensity by a masterful storyteller. They are best used in the 'shared reading' sessions where the teacher can lift the text off the page, explain, interpret, draw out meanings and encourage discussion of storyline and character. The more able reader will enjoy the challenge of the lively and imaginative text.

8. Who's Talking? *by Jean Ure, Orchard Books*

Two carefully illustrated stories for 7–9 year olds: short, very readable and by an excellent, sympathetic writer for children.

9. Harold and Bella, Jammy and Me *by Robert Leeson, Hamish Hamilton*

A collection of amusing tales, set in the North of England, about four unusual children and their adventures.

10. Tilly Mint Tales *by Berlie Doherty, Fontana*

An absolutely sure-fire collection of short stories. Amusing, good-hearted, gripping and verbally inventive, this collection is ideal for reading aloud. All Berlie Doherty's novels and stories are worth reading.

Some more story recommendations

- *Blue Shoes* by Angela Bull (ISBN 0 19918514 X);
- *Hamper's Great Escape* by Pippa Goodhart (ISBN 0 19918511 5);
- *Robbie Woods and his Merry Men* by Michaela Morgan (ISBN 0 19918513 1);
- *Heckedy Peg* by Don and Audrey Wood (ISBN 0 85953344 1);
- *Super Dad* by Shoo Rayner (ISBN 0 750002693 6);
- *Tell Tale Tom* by Ann Forsyth (ISBN 0 75001452 0);
- *The Magical Story House* by Adele Geras (ISBN 0 75001883 6);

- *Mr Cool Cat* by Rebecca Lisle (ISBN 0 75002675 8);
- *Hullaballoony* by Catherine Robinson (ISBN 0 75002661 8);
- *Jessica* by Christine Leo (ISBN 1 87051636 2);
- *Boots for a Bridesmaid* by Verna Allette Wilkins (ISBN 1 87051630 3);
- *Giant Hiccups* by Jacqui Farley (ISBN 1 87051627 3);
- *The Forgotten Garden* by Caroline Repchuk (ISBN 1 89878409 4).

Ten collections of myths and legends

> Myths and legends may seem remote from the child, but they will appeal to children at a level beyond concrete understanding and are well worth telling to any age group. The central metamorphosis and the moment of critical action will certainly linger in the imagination.
>
> (Jones and Buttrey 1970)

Myths are usually ancient traditional stories of gods and heroes concerned with the origins of life and death. The story of Persephone, the daughter of Zeus, for example, is a Greek myth, as is the tale of Prometheus. Persephone spent half the year on Earth and six months in the Underworld. Prometheus made men from the clay in the ground, taught them many arts and gave them fire, which he stole from heaven. A legend usually tells of the making of a nation through the exploits of its heroes. Legends like those of Robin Hood, King Arthur and Beowulf are said to be based on truth but have been exaggerated over the years. They are tales of daring deeds, fast action, strong emotion and are peopled by larger-than-life characters who show great courage, perseverance in the face of adversity, and a nobility of spirit.

1. The Dreamfighter *by Ted Hughes, Faber and Faber*

Ted Hughes is better known for his poetry but he can tell a captivating tale as those who have read *The Iron Man* and *The Iron Woman* will know. In this colourful collection of creation stories we are introduced to a clever, scheming and sometimes mischievous God, working hard to fashion his creatures and breathe life into them. He has some wonderful successes but sometimes there are a few mistakes. *How the Whale Became and Other Stories* is another carefully written and inventive collection of creation myths. Here, Hughes tells how each of the animals became as we know them today. Long ago when the world was new all the creatures were alike but with a little practice they became altogether different. In *Tales of the Early World*, God appears as a brilliant artist who is sometimes a little surprised by the creatures he makes. 'Some things take an awful lot of work,' He sighs. 'But others – they just seem to turn up.' The stories offer superb models for children's own creation myths.

2. The Puffin Classic Myths and Legends
by Roger Lancelyn-Green, Puffin

Beautifully and concisely retold, the stories of the Trojan Wars are brought to life with all the excitement, intrigue and drama. Tales of epic heroism like that of King Arthur are simply and poetically told and the text is enhanced by the superb woodcuts. This is a useful text for teaching children to recognise the elements of myths and legends and identify and describe characters and their relationships. The collection offers an excellent stimulus for a range of written, artistic and dramatic activities.

3. Tales from the Arabian Nights, *New Orchard*

The magic and mystery of Aladdin, Ali Baba and Sinbad are captured in this wonderfully colourful and varied collection. Thirty colour artworks by A. E. Jackson embellish the text. Some children will have been to pantomimes, seen the larger-than-life characters on stage and know a deal of background information about the stories. This gives the teacher a good opportunity to introduce this text and whet the appetite: discussing the cover, illustrations and titles and also encouraging the children to share their views and knowledge before tackling the stories.

4. Greek Myths for Younger Children *by Marcia Williams, Walker Books*

Marcia Williams devises an inventive way of retelling the myths of Orpheus, Perseus and other Greek heroes and introducing them to small children. She presents them in the style of a comic strip. The very funny and detailed cartoon illustrations are guaranteed to capture their imagination. This collection is suitable for the less able older reader to help him or her to learn about the Greek myths in a very enjoyable and accessible way. The teacher might follow up a 'guided reading' session, using this text, with some directed writing activities, allowing the children to recall, revise, consolidate and develop their understanding of a story by setting a series of simple questions or asking them to briefly retell a myth or write a short character description.

5. The Orchard Book of Creation Stories *by Margaret Mayo, Orchard Books*

A fascinating collection of inventive tales from around the world, each one drawn from a different culture. There are West African, North American Indian, Polynesian, Eskimo, Aborigine, Scandinavian, Egyptian and Central American tales, which explain just how things happen and why. Discover how the first man popped out of a peapod in Alaska, why the Central American monkeys look like human beings, how fire, in the North American Indian story, was hidden in the trees and why, in the Scandinavian story, the sea is so salty. Children will enjoy inventing their own creation myths, illustrating them and presenting them to the class.

6. Tales of Robin Hood *by Tony Allan, Usborne*

This is a bright and fast-moving collection of tales about the most famous of legendary Englishmen, his band of merry men, the beautiful Maid Marian and his arch enemy, The Sheriff of Nottingham. The text is lively, clear and very readable and the illustrations enhance the story well. The author provides a fascinating historical context to the adventures in Sherwood Forest and gives details of the many film versions. The collection, with the interesting background information, affords the teacher a good opportunity to explore the legend of Robin Hood and relate it to the historical facts and the period when he lived.

7. The Story of King Arthur *by Robin Lister, Kingfisher*

The classic tales of Sir Lancelot and the Knights of the Round Table are retold with verve and imagination. This collection is an excellent stimulus for discussion and drama.

8. Myths of the Norsemen *by Roger Lancelyn-Green, Puffin*

This unusual collection is full of heroes, fast action and fascinating descriptions, all of which will appeal to children, particularly boys. The tales offer a valuable resource for initiating discussion about the nature of myths and their relation to the historical facts about the Vikings. They also offer an exciting stimulus for writing and drama. Children, for example, might be asked to make a chart showing the features of each character and his or her relationship to the others, write a detailed description of a Viking, a vivid description of the Viking Homeland, a factual account of the Viking lifestyle, a clear factual description of the Viking longboat or a Norse riddle.

9. The King of Ireland's Son *by Brendan Behan, Andersen Press*

The King of Ireland sends his three sons, Art, Neart and Ceart, to discover the source of the heavenly music which can be heard the length and breadth of the land. For the one who finds out from where the music comes, half the kingdom will be his. The youngest prince, tricked by his elder brothers, finds a beautiful maiden held captive by an ogre and it is she who is making the heavenly music. This captivating retelling of a traditional Irish legend is full of rich imagery, amusing characters and lively dialogue and is illustrated by the Kate Greenaway prizewinning medallist, PJ Lynch. This is an excellent text for using in shared and guided reading sessions. Children might be asked to discuss the title, read the first page and predict what will happen, discuss the illustrations, read the entire book independently, note any unusual or difficult words and any interesting descriptions to talk about later.

10. The Orchard Book of Greek Myths *by Geraldine McCaughrean, Orchard Books*

This extremely well-written collection of 16 favourite Greek myths includes the heroic exploits of Jason, Theseus and Odysseus, of Icarus, who flies too close to the sun, Perseus, Heracles and King Midas, whose touch turns everything into gold. Lesser known myths are also included: Atlanta, the fleet-footed goddess, Arachne, the spinner, who boasts so much that she is turned into a spider and Narcissus, the vain shepherd boy who stares at his own beautiful refection and who pines away in hopeless love until he takes root and all that remains are 'the tissuey petals and a bending stalk'.

Some more recommendations

- *King Arthur*, retold by James Riordan (ISBN 0 19274177 2);
- *The Iliad*, retold by Barbara Leonie (ISBN 0 19274147 0);
- *The Odyssey*, retold by Barbara Leonie (ISBN 0 19274146 2);
- *An Ocean of Story, Tales from India*, retold by Caroline Ness (ISBN 0 75001688 4);
- *Norse Myths* by Kevin Crossley-Holland (ISBN 0 750001460 1);
- *Ivanhoe* by Andrew Skilleter (ISBN 0 19274146 2);
- *Celtic Myths*, retold by Sam McBratney (ISBN 075001813 5);
- *Dragons and Monsters* by Anita Ganeri (ISBN 0 7500 1814 3);
- *Five Heavenly Emperors: Chinese Myths of Creation* by Song Nan Zhang (ISBN 0 88776338 3).

Ten classic novels for older readers

The great story can change children's ways of looking at the world and at themselves; but poor story writers often have more influence, in the short run, on children's style because their conventions are mechanical and easily borrowed. In the long term, the quality of children's reading will certainly influence their writing.

(DES 1967)

1. The Adventures of Tom Sawyer *by Mark Twain, Viking*

Tom Sawyer, first published in 1876, is the enduringly popular tale of the irrepressible small-town boy growing up in the South at the time of the American Civil War. The novel is filled with memorable scenes: Tom tricking his pals to whitewash the fence, his friendship with the unconventional Huck Finn, his courtship of the pretty Becky Thatcher, his pursuit by the evil 'Injun Joe' and the exciting discovery of the hidden treasure. This is a story full of action and suspense and wonderfully drawn, memorable characters. Simplified versions and guided readers never succeed in capturing the linguistic richness of the original story. This edition is the complete and unabridged text but the reader is helped through the story by the generous annotations, captions and explanations of history, popular culture, geography and customs. It is lavishly illustrated with drawings, diagrams, maps and paintings. Other classic novels published in this series, and which would be valuable additions to any school book stock, include

Around the World in Eighty Days, The Call of the Wild, Heidi, The Jungle Book and *Treasure Island.*

2. **The Railway Children** *by E. Nesbit, Heinemann*

Roberta, Peter and Phyllis move with their mother from their big London house into a cramped little cottage near to the railway line. This is a novel peopled by memorable characters, exciting incidents, lively and authentic dialogue and is full of period details and atmosphere. E. Nesbit has succeeded in capturing the imaginations of children for a hundred years. There are several editions on the market but the Heinemann version has a mixture of black-and-white and colour illustrations which enhance the text and capture the period well.

3. **Swallows and Amazons** *by Arthur Ransome, Red Fox*

Set in the Lake District, this stirring tale of adventure is the first in a series about two families: The Walkers and the Blacketts. The four children in the novel are independent and resourceful and spend their summers camping on Wild Cat Island playing pirates and sailing. When they challenge the town children to prove their seamanship, the real adventure begins. There are strong story lines, a great deal of humour, many rounded characters and careful descriptions in Arthur Ransome's novels and they offer excellent texts for using in the Literacy Hour to examine with children the language and structure of a carefully-crafted story and for investigating the author's point of view.

4. **The Wind in the Willows** *by Kenneth Grahame, Penguin*

The delightful story of Ratty, Toad and Badger, tells of their adventures along the river bank and their skirmishes with the weasels and the stoats. There are many editions of this classic tale but two of the best are published by Methuen and Gollancz, where talented artists have interpreted the story superbly. The Penguin edition, however, is for me the best, and deserves a place in every classroom. The sixty wonderfully funny sketches by John Burningham add to the charm of this unforgettable tale.

5. **Alice in Wonderland** *by Lewis Carroll, Hutchinson*

The surreal and very funny story of Alice and her strange and wonderful adventures, is a must for all children. This classic story contains some of the best-loved and most bizarre characters in children's literature. There are many superb editions including those published by Julie MacRae, Orchard, Dragon's World and Gollancz but my favourite is the Hutchinson edition with its carefully crafted paintings on every page. Peter Weevers, the illustrator, used his own daughter as the model for Alice.

6. **Moonfleet** *by J. M. Faulkner, Puffin*

Moonfleet has all the ingredients of a rollicking adventure story: smugglers, buried treasure, hidden passages, shipwrecks, exciting chases along the beach and a dreadful curse. This is a compelling story of fast action and chilling menace and is full of the atmosphere of eighteenth century England. The novel is inaccessible for the less-fluent reader because of the detailed and sometimes complex language, but it is worth reading aloud or using extracts to show children how a master storyteller weaves a fast-moving and gripping story.

7. The Secret Garden *by Frances Hodgson Burnett, Michael Joseph*

Mary Lennox, spoilt, bad-tempered and lonely, comes to live with her reticent and reclusive uncle in a rambling isolated house in the middle of rural Yorkshire. Here she discovers a secret garden and another spoilt, bad-tempered and lonely child. This is a gripping story, sensitively-written with great warmth and authentic detail. There are several editions on the market: Puffin, Gollancz and Heinemann have produced attractive books enhanced by illustrations. The best is published by Michael Joseph and contains beautifully coloured and sepia illustrations and little detailed decorations interspersed in the text.

8. Little Women *by Louisa M. Alcott, Puffin*

First published in 1868, this engrossing story is about four sisters growing up at the time of the American Civil War and facing the hardships, anxieties and disappointments which came with it. There is a good strong storyline, plenty of tension and some wonderfully drawn characters.

9. Peter Pan *by J. M. Barrie, Viking Kestrel*

The enchanting story is about the Darling children who fly to Never-Never Land with Peter Pan, the boy who never grows up. Barrie is a compelling storyteller who takes the reader with him into a world of Indians and pirates, a world where the murderous Captain Hook searches for his age-old enemy, Peter Pan and lives in dread of the ticking crocodile that took his hand. This edition is the complete text, superbly enhanced by the illustrations of Jan Ormerod.

10. Black Beauty *by Anna Sewell, Gollancz*

Originally written to highlight the way in which horses were cruelly treated, this is arguably the best loved of all animal stories and can still claim a place on every library shelf. The dramatic story of the remarkable horse and the gentle child is told in a simple, direct and poignant way. This edition contains a mixture of black and white, half colour and full colour illustrations by the master illustrator, Charles Keeping.

Some more classic novels for older readers include

- *Moby Dick*, retold by Geraldine McCaughrean (ISBN 0 192781537 7);
- *Don Quixote*, retold by Michael Harrison (ISBN 0 19274182 9);
- *Gulliver's Travels*, retold by James Riordan (ISBN 0 19274178 0);
- *Canterbury Tales*, retold by Geraldine McCaughrean (ISBN 0 19274181 0);
- *El Cid*, retold by Geraldine McCaughrean (ISBN 0 19274169 1).

Ten short story collections for older readers

Short stories, by their very brevity and spareness of build are often more suitable for discussion than novels are. In stories you will find many details that deserve to be looked at closely. These details – crucial words and sentences, pivotal incidents, speeches and motives – can be related to theme, intention, attitude, criticism of life, to show how these abstractions are embodied in the story.

(Barnes and Egford 1973)

1. **The Ceremony and Other Stories** *by Martyn Copus, Fontana Lions*

Seven very funny stories, full of verbal wit, true-to-life characters, amusing escapades and clever surprises, all of which are guaranteed to keep the reader's attention. The stories centre on Terry, who is forever using his imagination and finding himself up to his neck in trouble. Of course, Tony, his best friend, is always there to suggest new ideas and adventures. The first story, in which Terry, to be one of the gang, has to pass the dreaded initiation ceremony, will make the reader laugh out loud. Simply written, gripping and hilariously funny and with clever twists at the end, these stories will ensure a lot of laughs. This is an excellent collection which will appeal to boys in particular and is ideal for demonstrating how good quality, short story writing is constructed.

2. **The Usborne Book of Spinechillers** *by Phil Roxbee Cox, Usborne*

Forty eight very readable and accessible stories packed with suspense and twists. Each spooky tale is illustrated with colourful pictures and in each there are clues and red herrings to keep the reader's interest.

3. **A Northern Childhood** *by George Layton, Longman*

A Northern Childhood is a warm and readable collection written in a lively, conversational style. The stories are based on the writer's own childhood experiences in Bradford where he grew up in the 1950s. Amusing storylines, strongly drawn characters, authenticity and humour characterise these very funny, often touching and always optimistic stories about boys growing up in a northern city.

4. **Apricots at Midnight** *by Adele Geras, Hamish Hamilton*

Set in Edwardian times, these ingenious stories are linked by the various materials which are used to make Aunt Pinny's patchwork quilt. Adele Geras is a powerful writer able to create a strong atmosphere, plenty of suspense and compelling characters.

5. **A Thief in the Village and Other Stories** *by James Berry, Penguin*

This bright, bubbly and very readable collection captures all the atmosphere of the author's native Jamaica. Each story portrays children with genuine warmth and understanding. The challenging and absorbing tales are full of endearing, strongly-drawn characters and are ideal for teachers wishing to encourage children to write character descriptions.

6. The Best Stories of William Saroyan, *Laurence Pollinger*

This delightful and intriguing collection of tales by the renowned American short story writer are down-to-earth, enjoyable and very accessible. In *The Great Leapfrog Contest*, Rosie Mahoney, the subject of the short story, is clever, crafty and tough. She fights the boys and most times wins and she is better than any of them at football, baseball and hockey. All this is too much for the leader of the gang, who decides to show everybody that he, for one, is not going to be beaten by a mere girl. These are splendid stories to initiate discussion with older juniors and to stimulate a range of writing.

7. The Turning Tide and Other Stories *edited by Gervase Phinn, Nelson*

A wide selection of lively writing by well known writers. Included in this anthology are stories by Joan Aiken, Gene Kemp, Berlie Doherty, Christine Bentley, David Harmer and Marjorie Kinnan Rawlings. There are funny, sad, contemplative, poignant and challenging stories which show the whole range of styles and structures. Imaginative follow-up activities are written at the back of the collection to encourage pupils to respond to the material and develop the National Curriculum requirements of reading, writing, listening and speaking. The ideas for writing offer individual, pair and group work ideal for Literacy Hour activities.

8. Ghost Dog *by Dick Cate, Gollancz*

Dick Cate, a teacher and writer for many years, knows exactly what kind of reading material will appeal to boys. His deep understanding of children enables him to write sincerely and directly for them. In this collection of lively, very readable and amusing stories, set in a Durham mining village, he creates an authentic world centred around the lives and interests of boys: football teams, the gang, friendships, family life and school. There is a genuine warmth and humour in these tales but they never become sentimental. The fast pace, clever storylines, lively dialogue and strong characterisation of the children enable boy readers to readily identify with these stories. Collections of stories like these are very satisfying for the reluctant boy reader who might find a novel hard going.

9. Tell Me a Story *edited by Eileen Colwell, Penguin*

A collection of stories compiled by one of the finest advocates of wide reading. Dr Eileen Colwell was a founder member of The Association of Children's Librarians and Chairman for five years of The International Federation of Library Associations. She was also a member of the Carnegie Medal Committee for many years. In *Tell Me a Story* she puts together a personal selection by a wide variety of writers, on different themes and in a range of styles. The stories are ideal for telling or reading aloud and for using in the Literacy Hour to teach about structure, characterisation, description, dialogue and significant detail.

10. **Warlock at the Wheel and Other Stories** *by Diana Wynne-Jones, Macmillan*

Diana Wynne-Jones is a splendid writer of intriguing and thought-provoking fantasy novels: *Archer's Goon, Cart and Cwidder, Charmed Life, Drowned Ammet, The Spellcoats* and many more. They are richly imaginative and beautifully written with well-drawn characters, excitement and a gentle thread of humour running through them. In this short story collection she creates a fascinating world in which the reader becomes totally engrossed.

Ten novels in different genres for older readers

There is no doubt at all in our minds that one of the most important tasks facing the teacher of older juniors is to increase the amount and range of their reading. We believe that there is a strong association between this and reading attainment.

(DES 1975)

1. *Ghost Story:* **The Ghost of Thomas Kempe** *by Penelope Lively, Penguin*

Strange things start happening in James's house. In trying to get to the bottom of the mysterious happenings he discovers a rather unusual ghost. Penelope Lively has written a number of novels where the past comes back to haunt the present – *The House in Norham Gardens, Astercote, The Driftway, The Revenge of Samuel Stokes* – and always succeeds in engaging the reader's interest.

2. *Fantasy:* **Wings** *by Terry Pratchett, Doubleday*

Like all Terry Pratchett's novels, this is one that boys in particular just cannot put down. It is a compelling fantasy story about a group of gnomes who live beneath a large department store soon to be razed to the ground. This is the tale of their epic journey to the Outside and the dangers that they meet.

3. *Mystery Story:* **The Dark Behind the Curtain** *by Gillian Cross, Hippo Books*

Things are not going too well at the rehearsals for the school play. There are mysterious goings on and the children are convinced that there is something sinister lurking behind the curtains. This is a gripping read with a strong storyline, wonderfully drawn characters and plenty of surprises, suspense and thrills.

4. *Science Fiction:* **Space Hostages** *by Nicholas Fisk, Puffin*

This novel has all the ingredients for an exciting and original story: strong plot, well-drawn characters, lively dialogue and plenty of suspense. A crazed and dying pilot, nine children and a top secret spacecraft and all of them out of control find themselves lost in space. Who will take charge? Brylo is the clever one but Tony is the strongest and nobody argues with Tony. This is a very readable and thought provoking story, written by a prolific and popular children's writer.

5. *Humorous Story:* The Turbulent Term of Tyke Tyler by Gene Kemp, Penguin

Children love Gene Kemp's books. Her stories are easy to read, original, full of amusing incidents and packed with lively characters who get up to all sorts of adventures and antics. The last term at primary school is a fraught time for the teachers, particularly when a certain class contains the notorious Tyke Tyler. This is an excellent novel to read out loud and serialise over a few sessions.

6. *Adventure Story:* The White Horse Gang *by Nina Bawden, Penguin*

Nina Bawden is a fine author who writes with a deep understanding of children. Her books have gripping plots and wonderfully drawn characters and contain a richness of language well worth studying. In this novel a group of lively children who need money for a good cause, kidnap the son from a very wealthy family and demand a ransom. Things do not work out quite as they expected and there is a thrilling development of the story and an exciting climax. This is an excellent text to demonstrate to children how a good writer uses a range of techniques to build up tension. It is also a useful novel to show young writers how to use significant detail in writing and draw rounded realistic characters.

7. *Historical Story:* The Eagle of the Ninth *by Rosemary Sutcliff, Puffin*

Rosemary Sutcliff is a writer of enormously powerful stories who introduces children to demanding and complex subjects and stirs up deep feelings. In this beautifully written novel, Roman Britain comes alive. A soldier begins his dangerous, lonely journey North to find out what happened to the lost legion and bring back the standard of the Eagle. This is another text useful for showing children how to build up suspense in a story, create believable characters and use vivid detail and description.

8. *Sport Story:* Tiger of the Track *by Michael Hardcastle, Magnet*

This is the sequel to another very readable short novel, *Roar to Victory.* Lee has to face a new challenge when his elder brother says he is a weakling. Determined to prove his brother wrong, he decides to ride on the toughest motorcycle circuit in Britain. Michael Hardcastle is a prolific writer of sports stories which will appeal to reluctant boy readers in particular. The pace is fast, the plots action-packed and the language very accessible.

9. *School Story:* Dear Mr. Henshaw *by Beverly Cleary, Penguin*

One of the finest American writers for children, Beverly Cleary writes with verve and imagination and creates warm-hearted, original stories and memorable characters. In this novel, written in the form of a series of letters, Leigh writes to a favourite author and soon they are corresponding regularly. This is an interesting text to use as a model for children's own writing and offers lots of possibilities for oral and drama work.

10. *War Story:* Goodnight Mr. Tom *by Michelle Magorian, Kestrel*

An extraordinary book full of superb characters, crackling dialogue and a fascinating plot. Willie Beech, evacuated from London, is billeted on the strong-minded, bad-tempered, and humourless Mr. Tom. The lonely child and the crusty old man develop a warm, gentle relationship which brings tears to the eye. This is a beautifully written novel and ideal for studying in some detail over a period of time.

Ten poetry anthologies

> Good poetry does undoubtedly tend to form the soul and character; it tends to beget a love of beauty and of truth in alliance together; it suggests, however indirectly, high and noble principles of action, it inspires the emotion so helpful in making principles operative. Hence its extreme importance to all of us; but in our elementary schools its importance seems to me at present quite extraordinary.
>
> (Arnold 1890)

1. Of Caterpillars, Cats and Cattle , Poems About Animals *chosen by Anne Harvey, Viking Kestrel*

Classic and contemporary poems which look afresh at the world of animals make up this varied anthology. There are cosy and amusing poems, poems which disturb and challenge and some beautifully quiet and descriptive verse.

2. Island of the Children, an Anthology of New Poems *compiled by Angela Huth, decorations by Jane Ray, Orchard Books*

The poems in this collection vary in style and subject and are all previously unpublished. Angela Huth wrote to over 100 poets and published their responses in this splendidly rich and original collection. There are poems of different lengths, moods and subjects, by well-known poets and unknown writers, each one generously printed and beautifully illustrated.

3. Lizard Over Ice *edited by Gervase Phinn, Nelson*

This anthology contains over 150 exciting and largely unfamiliar poems including haiku, jokes, chants and charms, epitaphs, ballads, acrostics, concrete poems and riddles. Poems modern and traditional come from Europe and Africa, the Caribbean, America and the Far East. Some of the poems have been written by children.

4. Madwhale, Miniwhale and Other Shape Poems *chosen by Wes Magee, Viking Kestrel*

Wes Magee was a primary head teacher and is a favourite children's writer. He chooses and writes poems which often reflect experiences in the classroom and he knows well which will be sure-fire successes with children. This collection of fascinating and original shape poems will inspire children to write their own. Frog spawn, pogo sticks, stars, hearts, telephone wires, worms, whirlpools and balloons cover page after page in this delightfully inventive anthology.

5. A New Treasury of Poetry *compiled by Neil Philip, Blackie*

A rich collection of popular and traditional verse from Australia, New Zealand, the Caribbean and elsewhere. Ted Hughes, Charles Causley, Philip Larkin, Rudyard Kipling, Robert Graves and many, many more poets rub shoulders in this stimulating anthology. Put together in 98 thematic sections, the anthology has a good balance of the serious and the comic, the formal and the informal, the immediate and the contemplative.

6. Ink Slinger *edited by Morag Styles and Helen Cook, A. and C. Black*

Poets such as John Agard, Seamus Heaney, Roger McGough, Wendy Cope, Judith Wright, Philip Larkin and many others, tell us how ideas become words and words become poems. Caroline Holden's lively line drawings enhance the text.

7. The Kingfisher Book of Children's Poetry *selected by Michael Rosen, Kingfisher Books*

A comprehensive collection of sad, funny, moving and powerful poems, produced in clear print with bold, bright illustrations. There are traditional favourites, ballads, lyrics, patterned poems, riddles and nonsense verses and many more. 'What you have in this book,' writes Michael Rosen, 'are hundreds of thoughts, dreams and ideas trapped in words for you to read, say or sing.' The companion volume, *The Kingfisher Book of Comic Verse*, edited by Roger McGough, incorporates all kinds of verse from the witty to the bizarre, the subtly amusing to the hilarious.

8. Mother Gave a Shout *edited by Susanna Steele and Morag Styles, A. and C. Black*

A treasure house of dynamic and diverse verse by women and girls from all over the world. Rhymes, jingles, lullabies, ancient poems of praise and celebration, funny, mysterious, reflective poems are enhanced by the simple, unobtrusive line drawings by Janet Ray.

9. The Walker Book of Poetry for Children *edited by Jack Prelutsky and Arnold Lobel, Walker Books*

Six hundred poems are packed into this big, bright, lively collection of traditional and contemporary verse. Arranged in 14 thematic sections, it includes children's rhymes, many different verse forms and some of the very best modern poetry. Another superb collection edited by Jack Prelutsky, *Read-Aloud Rhymes for the Very Young*, is a valuable resource for the nursery and infant classroom.

10. The New Golden Land Anthology *edited by Judith Elkin, Puffin*

This challenging and refreshing anthology of largely humorous stories and poems, ranges from Wordsworth to Michael Rosen, from Greek myths to Ted Hughes. The superb illustrations add to the book's wonder and delight.

Some further recommendations for poetry anthologies

- *The Orchard Books of Poems*, chosen by Adrian Mitchell (ISBN 1 86039268 7);
- *Off to School*, compiled by Tony Bradman (ISBN 0 7500 2150 0);
- *A Pale Horseman*, selected by Morag Styles (ISBN 0 60226148 1);
- *Strawberry Drums*, compiled by Adrian Mitchell (ISBN 0 75000364 2);
- *The Hairy Hamster Hunt and Other Pet Poems*, compiled by Tony Bradman (ISBN 0 7500 2662 6);
- *Word Whirls*, edited by John Foster (ISBN 0 19 27661889 9);
- *Crack Another Yolk*, edited by John Foster (ISBN 0 19276169 2);
- *Poems About Animals*, collected by Brian Moses (ISBN 0 75022438 X);
- *Excuses, Excuses*, compiled by John Foster (ISBN 0 19276151 X);
- *Let's Celebrate: Festival Poems,* compiled by John Foster (ISBN 0 19276083 1).

Ten individual poetry collections

Poetry matters because it is a central example of the use human beings make of words to explore and understand. It lends shape and meaning to our experiences and helps us to move with confidence in the world we know and then to step beyond it, to respond to the generation of meaning through significant, memorable and deliberated kinds of language.

(DES 1987)

1. Ask a Silly Question *by Irene Rawnsley, Methuen*

Brimming with laughter and fun, this delightfully inventive collection is full of sparkling language and shrewd insight. Written around four themes: *Me and My Family, In School, In the Playground* and *Out and About,* this collection is a must for the primary classroom. Teachers will smile as they recognise children like Tracey Johnson, the *Teacher's Pet* and Jonathan, the *Copycat* and children will laugh loudly at *A Nut up my Nose* and *Changing Places.*

2. Third Time Lucky *by Mick Gowar, Viking Kestrel*

With spontaneous freshness, Mick Gowar conjures up the brightest and clearest pictures of family life, school and the wide world around us. He has a real insight into and understanding of the feelings and thoughts of children and captures their imagination in his observant and original collection. The experience described in *Barry,* a poem about the surreptitious school bully, is one with which many children will identify.

3. Thawing Frozen Frogs *by Brian Patten, Viking*

An imaginative and varied sequel to *Gargling With Jelly*, this collection is excellent for introducing children to the whole range of poetry: sad and serious verse like *Aphasia* sits alongside manic and hilarious poems like *The Utter Butter Nutter*. Children love the sound, speed, action and humour of Brian Patten's poetry.

4. Complete Poems for Children *by James Reeves, Heinemann*

This is an attractive, mixed collection deliberately chosen to cover both old and new, familiar and unfamiliar, easy and difficult. These musical, haunting, thought-provoking poems will excite, challenge and inspire children who hear them.

5. Hot Days and Other Poems *by Kit Wright, Puffin*

Here are poems which cover a wide range of themes and emotions; poems about things we like and things we hate, familiar sayings and daily events. Kit Wright's excellent verse has all the qualities which appeal to children: lively language, a sense of drama, strong regular rhythms, echoing rhymes and originality of expression.

6. Standing on a Strawberry *by John Cunliffe, Andre Deutsch*

Written by the author of the *Postman Pat* books, this amusing, warm-hearted, funny collection provides lots of reading and listening fun for children. There are noisy boys and quiet girls, strict head teachers and loveable teachers, typical mums and unusual dads, grans and dentists and the forlorn pop star at 40 who has hung up his silver lurex. There are telephone poems, riddles, epitaphs, vigorous rhymed verse and some sadly perceptive poems but all are guaranteed to captivate and offer excellent models for the children's own poetry writing.

7. Classroom Creatures *by Gervase Phinn, Roselea Publications*

Meet *The Little Chatterbox* who has a particular way with words, join mum and dad on *Parents' Evening*, go along on the *School Trip* to Scarborough, eavesdrop on the *Interrogation in the Nursery*, read the *Letter to the Headteacher* and meet a whole collection of children, parents, teachers and the dreaded school inspectors. All those involved in the education of the young will recognise the delights and disasters of everyday life in school. Illustrated with panache by Matthew Phinn.

8. Mind Your Own Business *by Michael Rosen, Fontana Lions*

No classroom or library poetry collection would be complete without a selection of Michael Rosen's verse. This poet has done more than any to make poetry accessible to young readers. His rhythms, rhymes, images and ideas are irresistible. Children delight in his warm humour, love the catchy rhymes and identify with the moods and feelings he so skilfully captures.

9. The Jungle Sale *by June Crebbin, Viking Kestrel*

Children and teachers will find much to entertain and amuse them in this very accessible and sympathetic collection about school, family and holidays. Meet Jimmy who comes out in spots and gets sent home, find out how to have a gerbil's funeral, discover what happens when a crocodile visits the local swimming pool, learn how to do joined-up writing and hear about the trials and tribulations of the *Silk-Moth Monitor*. June Crebbin has a fine understanding of children's feelings and a real ear for the language of the classroom and playground.

10. Big Billy *by Peter Dixon, Sarsen Press*

Children love the humour, cleverness of language, the rhymes and rhythms of Peter Dixon's vibrant verse. Wild, wonderful and exaggerated characters abound on page after page. There is *Big Billy*, the spider with legs as thick as a rope and *Bertie Fly* who no-one likes. There's *Jeffthebreath*, the hold-your-breath champion and *Mr. Brown Nose of Cuckoo Farm*. Offbeat, amusing and original, this collection is enhanced superbly by the quirky and endearing illustrations of David Thomas. In addition to his poetry collections Peter Dixon had produced ten superbly illustrated poster poems ideal for use in the Literacy Hour.

Some further recommendations for individual poetry anthologies

- *Michael Rosen's Book of Nonsense* by Michael Rosen (ISBN 0 705002192 6);
- *Balloon Lagoon* by Adrian Mitchell (ISBN 1 84121119 2);
- *Fizzy Whizzy Poetry Book* by John Cunliffe (ISBN 0 59013160 5);
- *Give Yourself a Hug* by Grace Nichols (ISBN 0 140372180 0);
- *Smile Please!* by Tony Bradman (ISBN 0 14032286 8);
- *An Imaginary Menagerie* by Roger McGough (ISBN 0 140327908);
- *Junk Mail* by Michael Harrison (ISBN 09 19276113 7);
- *Green Poems* by Jill Bennett (ISBN 0 19276198 6);
- *The Worst Class in School* by Brian Moses (ISBN 0 75022540 8);
- *Making Friends with Frankenstein* by Colin McNaughton (ISBN 0 74454321 5);
- *The House That Caught A Cold* by Richard Edwards (ISBN 0 6708835883 8).

Ten non-fiction books

There is a massive range of non-fiction books now available, written specifically with children in mind. There are comprehensive guides to history, geography, art, music and the world of science and also engrossing and very readable texts on more esoteric subjects like philosophy and astronomy. There are books on every conceivable subject from incredible insects to dangerous dinosaurs. The following reference books are all 'unstuffy', brightly illustrated, innovative and bring the information to life in a clear, concise and entertaining way.

1. The Children's Illustrated Bible *retold by Selina Hastings, Dorling Kindersley*

The best loved stories of the Old and New Testaments are retold in a lively and very accessible way. The author captures well some of the poetry, the drama and the richness of language of the Bible and the illustrations by Eric Thomas enhance the text superbly.

2. Keeping Clean: A Very Peculiar History *by Daisy Kerr, Watts Books*

This is the third book in a fascinating series which includes *Mummies, Underwear* and *Vanity*. In this superbly illustrated and clearly written volume, the author gives a very public account of a very private subject. From Ancient Roman sponge sticks to Viking ear-wax removers, from medieval bath houses to the 264 commodes of Versailles, from the monks' multi-seater lavatory to the astronauts' space funnels – we learn all about ablutions through the ages.

3. Anne Frank: Beyond the Diary *by Rudd van der Rol and Rian Verhoeven, Puffin*

The Diary of Anne Frank is a must for all older children and this companion volume, with superb photographs and clear, simple text, helps the young reader to understand about Anne's life and the frightening world in which she lived. Another book by these fine writers is *Dear Anne Frank*, a series of letters written to Anne by children today. The letters are moving, perceptive and thoughtful and can lead to some lively discussions about Anne's world compared to the world as it is today.

4. Incredible Cross-Sections *by Stephen Biesty, Dorling Kindersley*

Children will spend hours looking though this fascinating book and studying the highly detailed cross-sections of building and machines which range from a mediaeval cathedral to a Spanish galleon. It is full of remarkable facts and figures and is guaranteed to intrigue. All the Dorling Kindersley books contain superb designs and stunning photographs which bring the world of non-fiction to life. Other books worth adding to the library collection are: *The Children's Encyclopaedia, The Eyewitness Atlas of the World, The Child's Book of Art* and *The Illustrated History of the World*.

5. World Religions Past and Present, *Moonlight Books*

A beautifully illustrated and clearly written volume which explores the core beliefs common to most religions: the existence of a supreme deity, faith, prayer, festivals, ceremonies and the mysteries of life and death. The beliefs of the Ancient Egyptians, Greeks and Celts are described and the oral and written traditions of many living religions are considered in this comprehensive, very readable book.

6. War Boy: A Country Childhood *by Michael Foreman, Puffin*

A vivid, informative and highly readable autobiography which gives the reader a feel for what it was like to be a boy growing up during the Second World War.

7. How Your Body Works, *Usborne Books*

Entertaining and instructive, this book explains the complicated and amazing functions of the human body. The print is clear and the illustrations clever and varied. A very colourful and readable companion volume, containing lively illustrations and informative diagrams, is *Understanding the Facts of Life* which approaches a tricky topic clearly and directly.

8. The History of Britain and Ireland *by Christopher Wright, Kingfisher Books*

The writing in this useful reference text is clear, vivid and very accessible. The book traces the history of the two countries from the early times to the present, and includes information about the daily life of the people as well as significant historical events. Photographs, paintings, sketches, maps and scenic reconstructions enhance the text.

9. Pictures of Home *by Colin Thompson, Julia MacRae*

This is an extraordinary collection of strange, beautiful, bizarre and captivating pictures, originally produced for the Leeds Permanent Building Society calendars. In this hardback edition the pictures have been linked to children's comments about their homes. Sometimes the children's observations are amusing ('What I really love about home is that you don't have to pay for your dinner'), sometimes touching ('Every home should have a heart'), sometimes quite philosophic ('Home is the world') but all have the honesty and the imagination of the young.

10. The Gaia Atlas of Planet Management *edited by Norman Myers, Pan Books*

A very useful reference book for the more able junior reader. It looks at how we humans use the Earth's vast resources and explains how, if we do not take care of the planet, the future is bleak. It is packed full of interesting facts, contains a wealth of data, diagrams, tables, statistics and vivid graphics.

Some further recommendations for non-fiction texts

- *Caves, Graves and Catacombs* (ISBN 1 86373929 7);
- *Soccer* (ISBN 1 86448085 8);
- *Mysterious Ruins* (ISBN 1 86373767 7);
- *The United Kingdom* (ISBN 0 75002613 8);
- *The Atlas of Ancient Greece and Ancient Rome* (ISBN 0 7500 2408 9);
- *The Atlas of the Bible Lands* (ISBN 0 7500 2633 2);

- *Rainforest* (ISBN 0 7500 2735 5);
- *What Do We Know About Religions?* (ISBN 0 7500 1981 6);
- *Tremendous Treks* (ISBN (0 7500 2504 2);
- *Fabulous Beasts* (ISBN 0 7500 2526 3);
- *Wonders of the World* (ISBN 0 7500 2584 0);
- *Ancient Egyptian People* (ISBN 0 7500 2033 4);
- *The Illustrated History of the World* (ISBN 0 75001524 1);
- *Space Shuttle* (ISBN 0 7500 2583 2);
- *The Roman Fort* (ISBN 0 19910426 3);
- *The Human Being* (ISBN 0 10910148 5);
- *The Oxford Children's Book of Famous People* (ISBN 0 19910599 5).

PART II

Chapter 4
Responding to Stories at Key Stage 1

Reading and telling stories aloud has always been a feature of infant education but recent research has shed new light on the process and its crucial role in early literacy development. What it seems to do is help children overcome considerable difficulties presented by the abstract nature of print. When adults read aloud with expression and gesture, they make the print 'come alive' and aid the comprehension of unusual language structures that are quite different from the kinds of language used in practical contexts and around everyday happenings.

(Burman 1990)

The National Literacy Strategy states that 'the successful teaching of reading involves frequent opportunities for pupils to hear, read and discuss text and to think about the content and the language used.' Presenting stories is an essential part of 'shared reading' and is invaluable in developing young children's understanding of the purpose of written language. It is also a powerful means of stimulating an interest in and excitement about books, encouraging children to talk and think about words and structures and helping them understand about plot, character, setting and themes. Over a term I presented a series of stories to infant children in the shared reading sessions. Some were read using a big book, with the children following the text and joining in when they felt confident. Some were told to the children in a storytelling session without any reference to a text. Others were read aloud by the teacher with the children listening or following in the text. My aims were to introduce the pupils to a rich range of written material and to:

- encourage them to listen attentively to a variety of stories and poems in a range of contexts;
- give them experience of reading and hearing stories and poems of their own choosing;
- make stories important and enjoyable for them;
- encourage them to actively participate in the reading when they felt confident to do so;
- stimulate their own spoken language, encouraging them to speak with clarity, confidence and expression;
- give them the opportunity to analyse the letter-sound relationships within words;

- teach them about the surface features of writing such as spelling and punctuation and draw their attention to the grammatical structure of written language;
- teach them explicitly about the nature of the reading process, including the value of thinking ahead, predicting, checking and self-correcting;
- help them understand how successful stories work;
- teach them about the typical conventions of early fiction – storyline, character and theme;
- give them the opportunity of having their speech written down as a resource for reading;
- foster their voluntary independent reading;
- foster their own writing.

A big book story (Reception/Year1): *Kangaroos* by Martin Waddell, illustrated by Frank James, Ginn

The children were gathered in a half circle on the carpet in the Reading Corner, sitting in a position where they were able to see the big book clearly.

- The class was shown the cover of the book and the children asked what they thought it would be about. Two large smiling kangaroos are seen bouncing along the street, kicking their legs high in the air and observed by a group of astonished onlookers.
- Title page, author and illustrator were introduced.
- I demonstrated how to turn the pages of the book without damaging it.
- A general discussion followed about kangaroos: if anyone had seen any, what did they look like, from which country did they come, was there anything special about them? The children knew a surprising amount about kangaroos – that they carried babies in pouches, that they could jump long distances and that male kangaroos box each other.
- The text was introduced without giving too much of the story away.
- The first three pages of the book were read:

> Kate saw a small kangaroo
> On a trip to the zoo.
> 'I want one too!' said Kate.
> So she went to the shops and
> She bought herself one.
> It slept in the kitchen
> So that was all right.

- The children were asked to say what they thought would happen next.
- The story was read to the end with the children encouraged to join in when they felt confident to do so. I felt that it was important that the story should be appreciated and enjoyed before it was analysed.
- The story was reread and the children asked questions for me to assess their understanding. 'Why did the kangaroo feel at home in Kate's house?' 'How do

you think the cat felt about the kangaroo coming to stay?' 'What sort of things would the kangaroo eat?' 'What happened when the kangaroo played in the garden?' 'What did the neighbours do?'

- The text was interrogated in a sensitive way and used to teach certain skills and decoding strategies. Children were asked to supply rhymes for particular words, identify words beginning with a particular letter, talk about and spell out the key words, guess what certain words meant, supply alternatives for high frequency words like 'said', discuss the use of full stops, commas, exclamation marks and different font sizes, repetition and rhyme.
- The story was read by the teacher and the children for a third time. The children were encouraged to perform the story using techniques such as timing, expression, tone of voice, accent and intonation.
- The children were then asked to retell the story in the correct sequence. Each child was asked to draw a story sequence with captions.
- A big class mural was made based on the story with cut-out characters and simple text.

Sharing a big book with small children is undertaken in a non-competitive, good-humoured and supportive learning environment. The books selected need to be sufficiently interesting and challenging to be read and reread, they need to have a strong storyline, appeal to young children, have bright attractive illustrations and accessible language with plenty of repetition. It is important to have a rich selection of big books which include: nursery rhymes, traditional tales, short plays, songs, descriptions, recipes and other factual books and store them in a place where children can find them should they wish to reread them independently later on.

A story told (Years 1 and 2): *Lizzie's Mouse* by Gervase Phinn, Roselea Publications

This story, which takes about ten minutes to relate, was told to the children. It begins:

One Saturday morning in October, Lizzie was helping her grandpa in the garden. The leaves covered the grass in a carpet of reds and golds and browns. Fat green apples and round juicy pears hung from the fruit trees.

In Spring grandpa had planted small green cabbages, radishes, sprouts, cauliflower, carrots and beans and they had watched them grow and grow and grow in the dark earth.

In Summer Lizzie had helped grandpa dig up the long carrots, the flaky skinned onions and the bright green leeks which ended up in one of Grannie Bentley's famous stews. Lizzie would help Grandpa cut big bunches of brightly-coloured flowers and gather the juicy blackberries.

In Winter, when nothing grew, Lizzie built a snowman on the lawn. She gave her snowman a long carrot nose and two pebble eyes and scratched a long smiling mouth across the frozen face. Sometimes, when the dangling icicles hung like glistening knives from the roof of the shed, Lizzie would help her grandpa clear the icy path, their breath hanging in the air. She would watch the flakes of snow settle on the branches of the fruit trees and drift against Grandpa's coat and melt.

That Autumn Saturday morning, the air was cold and misty and Lizzie was by herself in the garden shed, sitting on one of Grandpa's old garden chairs drinking a hot cup of soup. Grannie had made a big flask of vegetable soup for them that morning to keep out the cold. Grandpa was outside busily raking up all the fallen leaves. Lizzie lifted the small plastic cup to her lips and she saw something out of the corner of her eye. It was a little movement near the sacks in the dusty darkness of the shed. There was a little scratching, then a scraping. Lizzie peered into the darkness and two small shiny eyes, like black beads, stared back at her. There was a skittering and a scuttling and whatever it was disappeared.

'We've got a mouse, Lizzie!' said Grandpa, as he locked up the shed later that day. 'There's a mouse in my shed.'

'How do you know, Grandpa?' asked Lizzie.

'Because something has been eating my seeds, nibbling though the paper I use to store my daffodil bulbs, chewing the cardboard boxes and eating some of those nuts I put on the bird table in Winter.'

'It might not be a mouse,' said Lizzie.

'Well, it's not an elephant, poppet,' chuckled Grandpa. 'It's a mouse all right, and I'm afraid I shall have to dispose of it.'

Lizzie knew what grandpa meant by 'dispose of it' and she was very sad.

The story traces the attempts of Grandpa to catch the mouse and Lizzie's efforts to stop him. All ends happily when Grandpa admits defeat and gives up.

'I think because he's so special,' said Grandpa smiling, 'we'll leave the little fellow alone. It would be a real pity to get rid of such a clever little mouse, don't you think, Lizzie? We'll just have to get along.' Lizzie gave her grandpa the biggest of biggest of hugs.

Following the storytelling the children were asked to:

- Relate the story to their own personal experiences.
- Retell the story simply in the correct sequence.
- Clarify explicit and implicit meanings by answering questions about essential elements in the story.
- Recall parts of the story and talk about some key moments.
- Discuss some of the features of the language used: description, detail and use of certain words. Key words were written on the whiteboard and the spelling discussed.
- Describe the characters and the relationship between them.
- Identify and describe the parts of the story they liked the best.
- Say what might happen next.
- Draw four seasonal pictures of Grandpa's garden – Spring, Summer, Autumn and Winter – with accompanying captions.
- Draw a series of story boards which follow the sequence of the story and provide beneath some simple written text. More able children were asked to retell the story in their own words.

Storytelling is a natural, shared, social activity much enjoyed by young children. By presenting a range of interesting stories and by using facial expressions, different accents and varying tones of voice, the teacher increases young children's familiarity with the language of stories and with the patterns and rhythms of the spoken word. Storytelling encourages careful listening and thinking and lively talking.

A story read (Years 1 and 2): *The Naughty Leprechaun of Oranmore* by Gervase Phinn in *Trouble at Blimpton Gap and Other Stories*, Kingscourt (to be republished by Roselea Publications)

> In the dark, wet slippery rocks near the great castle of Oranmore there lived a leprechaun called Sean. Sean was not an ordinary leprechaun. In fact he was very, very different from all the other fairy folk who lived thereabouts.

So begins the Irish fairy tale. Before reading the story the children were asked to look at the title page and make predictions about what the story might be about. We discussed the title, author information and illustrator.

Following a reading of the complete story, the children were asked to:

- Compare the story to other fairy stories they had heard. *The Naughty Leprechaun of Oranmore* is typical of the fairy tale. It has magic and fantasy, exaggerated characters, fast action, suspense, repetition of events and finally a happy ending where good triumphs over bad.

- Clarify their understanding by answering questions about essential elements in the story.
- Recall parts of the story and talk about some key moments.
- Discuss some of the features of the language used: description, detail and use of certain words.
- Describe the characters and the relationship between them. Discuss the beginning, development of the story and the ending.
- Talk about how the writer attempts to paint a picture in words of the beach, sea, cliffs, castle and the bog hole, using details, adjectives and description.
- Discuss the use of dialogue. The whiteboard was used here to show the children how direct speech is set out.
- Identify and describe the part of the story they liked best. Provide alternative endings.
- Draw the part of the story they liked best and add short captions.

Sharing a story in this way encourages the children to anticipate, predict and to identify structures, patterns and words. The teacher is able to point out aspects of the story as he or she reads, stopping at appropriate places to discuss events, characters, pictures and words. This 'modelling' develops children's understanding of the functions and the features of language and informs their own creative efforts. Hearing, reading and discussing a text combined with the explicit teaching about the content, structure and language, certainly had a very positive effect on the children's own writing and bears out what Roger Beard stresses and which was clearly recognised by the Cox Committee:

> Children can be helped to become elegant and imaginative writers by being encouraged to read widely and by being read to. What may not be so widely appreciated is the way in which teachers and parents can foster the growth in children's writing ability by regularly pointing out some of the features of the writer's finesse, so that children can read increasingly with a writer's alertness to technique.
>
> (Beard 1991)

> The process of reading should be an active experience, involving questioning, problem solving, hypothesising and imagining. By reading a wide range of literature children become aware of new forms of expression and modes of discourse with which they may experiment in their own writing.
>
> (DES 1988b)

Children were asked to respond to some of the books they had read by writing about them in their own personal way or in the form of a book review, poster, book jacket or advertisement, to inform others and persuade them to read what they themselves had found enjoyable. On occasion, stories were used as springboards. Here are some of the best efforts, all written by Key Stage 1 children.

Michael is a quiet and under-confident boy who has some difficulty with his reading and writing. His account (Figure 4.1) is a second draft. It is short and he uses words sparingly, but it is a delightful piece and demonstrates that this young child knows a great deal about the writing process. The account, written after hearing the story *Lizzie's Mouse*, has a clear intention – to communicate an incident which happened at home. It is well organised and structured – he has written from top to bottom and from left to right, leaves spaces between words, forms letters

I Law a mouse in my house. It stuck in my hoover and It scared my mum.

Figure 4.1 Michael's story, 'I saw a mouse … '

Wheh we had a Pizza My brother Dominic shirrred. Some Peffer It went up his nose and made him sneeze. He Will not do that Un a huury again.

Figure 4.2 Becky's visit to the pizza parlour

clearly and legibly, knows about lower and upper case letters, can punctuate and spell – and his piece is original and entertaining.

In this second piece (Figure 4.2) written after we read as a class the big book, *The Pizza Princess*, published by Ginn in the *All Aboard* series, Becky describes her family's ill-fated visit to the pizza parlour. This is her second draft, largely unchanged in content but written after some spellings had been corrected.

Debbie, is a very confident, independent and fluent reader who has been exposed in the home and at school to a wide range of appropriate texts. Her self-esteem as a reader and writer is very high and she spoke with confidence about her work. In this lively authentic account (Figure 4.3), a second draft, she demonstrates an unusual zest, freshness and originality, typical of all her work. It was written after reading *A Present for Paul* by Bernard Ashley, published by Collins in the *Picture Lions* series. Like Bernard Ashley this young writer sets the scene before confidently launching into the story. She organises her writing well, recounts the incident clearly and writes neatly. She also enhances the text, as writers of picture books do, with illustrations. In writing the first draft she was observed functioning as a very proficient reader making adjustments to her work, correcting spellings, checking words in her dictionary, adding punctuation and keeping track of the organisation of the narrative she was recounting.

Simon, in his observations about the school inspector (Figure 4.4), obviously has taken to heart the teacher's comment that the successful writer needs to be a good listener and have 'an ear for language'. This articulate, lively and interested boy hears stories and poems read regularly at home and in school and speaks with the blunt, disarming honesty of the young child.

Geoffrey's nose is never out of a book and he has a growing collection of novels, stories, poetry anthologies and non-fiction material in his bedroom. Most of the books he buys from the school bookshop. He finds the work he undertakes challenging and his account demonstrates the close interplay of reading and writing. In his first draft he was observed reading to find words he wanted to use and copying them out. He writes, edits, self-corrects and proof reads as all successful writers do. This superb, sharply observed and inventive account (second draft Figure 4.5) of the trip to the farm is full of surprises and sly humour. The text is organised extremely well, the writer employing a growing store of conventional spellings, at the same time guessing more unusual words. (notice his spelling of 'heifers'). He explores a range of punctuation and tries out apostrophes. Particularly interesting is the complexity of the grammar, the very sophisticated sentence structures and the clever ending.

Geoffrey, at such a young age, does something which all good writers do – he experiments in his writing, tries out new words, sentence structures and spellings. This experimentation is a vital part of becoming a successful language user. Judith Newman (1984) writes:

> Experimentation is essential for learning language. Every spoken exchange, each writing effort, represents an experiment: Is this what I mean to say? Do I say it this way or that? Are these the particular words I want to use? Consequently, learning to be a successful language user is a risky business...If no risks are taken, little can be learned.

Lost in Ripon

one day my mummy and daddy went to Ripon and I went too. Daddy went in a bookshop with the brothers and mummy went in a dress shop with me.

I hid in some coats. they could not find me. Mummy cried and Daddy paniced the brothers stood as still as stone after a few minites I popped out my head and said pepo you little horror said mummy.

Figure 4.3 Debbie's account 'Lost in Ripon...'

On Monday Mr Dabson came into school. He was fat with wiskers and a flat cap. He wouldeht stop talking. He got boring and we fell asleep. Mrs Wilson said he liked the sound of his own voice.

Figure 4.4 'On Monday Mr. Dobson . . .' by Simon

last xJx Tuesday we Went to Wilson's farm.
ny friendmark Was Sick on the Bus
all over the seat his Shoes his
cout and mrs Tomsen she Went mad
and Smelt horible. mark had to
put his head in a Big blue
plastic bucket mrs. Tomsen pulled
faces all the Way. When we
got to the farm mark trod
in Some cow pats mr Wilson
the the farmer said pooo Something smells worse than my
pigs. mrs Tomsen went bright
red. farmer Wilson showed us
Some horses and pigs and
Big cows and hens and
geese; then he pointed to
a feild. he said look at
those ff.ers but I couldént see
eny.

Figure 4.5 'Last Tuesday we went...' by Geoffrey

Debbie's and Geoffrey's writing was typed out accurately and used with other infant groups. Their accounts were enlarged on an overhead projector and the children followed as the teacher read them and talked about the structure, use of certain words, spellings and significant details. Presenting pupils' own work can be a very valuable and interesting part of 'shared reading' and is useful in developing children's understanding of the purpose of writing, stimulating them to compose their own stories and poems and encouraging them to talk and think about the language. Here is an outline of how Debbie's account was used. The children were asked to:

- Listen attentively and follow the reading as the teacher presented the account.
- Relate the story to their own personal experiences:
    Have they ever been lost? What happened? Where was it? What did you feel like? How do you think your parents felt? What did they say when you were found?
- Retell the story simply in the correct sequence.
- Clarify explicit and implicit meanings by answering questions about essential elements in the story. Recall parts of the story and talk about some key moments:
    Where did Debbie get lost? What was Mummy doing at the time? What was Daddy doing? How did Debbie come to be lost? What did Mummy do when she found Debbie had gone missing? What did Daddy do? What did the brothers do?
- Discuss some of the features of the language used: description, detail and use of certain words. Key words were written on the whiteboard and the spelling discussed.
    Can you describe a dress shop? Can you describe a bookshop? Why does Ripon have a capital letter? What does 'panicked' mean? What does 'as still as stone' mean? Can you think of some interesting words to describe how Debbie, her parents and her brothers felt after she went missing and when she was found? Why is 'popped' a better word that 'put'?
- Identify and describe the parts of the story they liked the best.
- Describe the characters and the relationship between them.
- Say what might happen next.
- Draw a series of story boards which follow the sequence of the story and provide beneath some simple written text. More able children were asked to retell the story with added details in their own words or write their own account.
- Discuss the beginning, development of the story and the ending.
- Discuss the use of dialogue. The whiteboard was used here to show the children how direct speech is set out.
    Notice how we set out the speech at the end of the account:
    I popped out my head and said, 'Peepo!'
    'You little horror!' said Mummy.

We learn to read and to write by experiencing language and by using it. Effective literacy teaching involves the constant reading of good quality texts, the sharing of ideas with others and the explicit teaching of how language works. The National Literacy Strategy defines the content of literacy instruction. It is not merely telling children how to read and write, it is about showing them. It spells out very clearly that the approach in the Literacy Hour should be 'wide ranging and should not be a passive process for children'. It involves:

- Directing
- Demonstrating
- Explaining
- Questioning
- Guiding
- Investigating
- Listening
- Observing
- Arguing
- Criticising
- Questioning
- Evaluating
- Assessing.

The Literacy Hour also involves challenging and exciting children about language. David Blunkett (1999), in a reply to his critics who claim that the Literacy Hour stifles creativity, maintains that it 'offers considerably more flexibility than its critics would allow.' He continues:

The reality is that as well as being taught to spell properly and learn the rules of grammar, the Literacy Hour enables children to learn poetry, prose, drama and other creative writing, with access to more texts than ever before.

Chapter 5

Responding to Stories at Key Stage 2

Literacy experiences must continue right through school; and reading aloud is vital. All children have the right to hear and know a story for pleasure and for their emotional and mental growth...A successful reader-aloud can help children learn to pace and respond to their own reading.

(Bennett 1982)

Performing a story

Children should be taught how to read a story aloud, how to lift the text from the page to captivate the listener, using the skills and techniques of a good presenter. I worked with three Year 6 groups and their teachers, teaching aspects of story performance. My aims were to introduce the children to a rich range of written material and:

- make stories more important and enjoyable for them;
- encourage them to read with confidence and use techniques such as timing, expression, tone of voice, accent and intonation;
- help them to talk with confidence about literature;
- encourage them to listen attentively in a range of contexts;
- develop in them an 'ear for language';
- stimulate their own spoken language, equipping them with the skills to speak with clarity, confidence and expression;
- teach them about the features of good quality writing and help them understand how successful stories work;
- foster their voluntary independent reading.

We did this through a combination of instruction, questioning, discussion, small group and paired activities. One of the most successful projects focused upon reading aloud and storytelling and related to the theme of *Time*. We chose this theme because there is an endless range of historical and science fiction short stories available with exciting themes, powerful narratives and interesting characters. We hoped that the children's study of history and science would be enhanced, deepened and brought alive by telling and reading stories about the past and the future, that their growing historical and scientific imaginations would be nourished and that the material would provide a rich background knowledge for their project work.

Storytelling and reading aloud to children open new and exciting worlds and help them make sense of their own experiences and feelings and those of others. They are rich learning experiences which not only reveal the rhythms, richness and variety of language, but also help children learn how to respond to narrative: to remember events, empathise with the characters, express their views, predict what might happen, appreciate humour and suspense. Through storytelling and reading aloud the teacher broadens children's experience of the spoken word, expands their appreciation of literature, helps them understand how stories work and offers good models for their own storytelling and story writing. The teacher is able to develop the children's understanding of significant themes, events and characters, help them locate and express ideas, experiences and opinions, infer, deduce, explain their views and develop a confidence and enthusiasm in speaking and concentration in listening.

Through their exposure to good quality stories, where the text is lifted from the page by a skilful reader, children also come to appreciate the importance of timing, expression, accent, tone of voice and body language.

The selection of the stories

Each teacher taking part in the project read, over the school holidays, a small selection of stories on the theme of *Time*. We met and compiled a booklist of the texts we felt would kindle in children an interest in the past and the future and develop important literacy skills. Sonia Benster was invaluable in suggesting appropriate stories for us to read and try out with the children. Also very useful were the following publications:

- *Stories in Time and Place*, published by Derbyshire School Library Service;
- *Stories for Time* by Chris Routh and Anne Rowe, Reading and Language Information Centre, The University of Reading;
- *More Stories for Time* by Chris Routh and Anne Rowe, Reading and Language Information Centre, The University of Reading;
- *Learning Through Stories*, Anglian Young Books;
- *Books for Boys*, published by The Shropshire County Council Community and Economic Services Department;
- *The Puffin Literacy Hour Booklist*, compiled by Wendy Cooling, Puffin.

We wanted a wide variety of short stories: historical and science fiction, fantasy and realistic, in a range of styles, from different cultures, some traditional and some modern. Many were ideal for reading aloud or performing because they had unusual settings, exaggerated characters, lively dialogue and fast action. Below is our final selection. Most of the collections from which they come are described in greater detail earlier on in the book.

1. *Extraterrestrials* by Ivor Baddiel and Tracy Blezard, Macdonald Young Books;
2. *Ghostly Tales from Long Ago* by Peter Hepplewhite and Neil Tonge, Macdonald Young Books;

3. *The Fib*, in *A Northern Childhood* by George Layton, Longman;
4. *The Great Leapfrog Contest*, in *The Best Stories of William Saroyan*, Laurence Pollinger;
5. *Butch* by Christine Bentley, in *The Turning Tide and Other Stories*, edited by Gervase Phinn, Nelson;
6. *Warlock at the Wheel*, in *Warlock at the Wheel and Other Stories* by Diana Wynne-Jones, Macmillan;
7. *The King of Ireland's Son* by Brendan Behan, Andersen Press;
8. *Three Indian Princesses: The Stories of Savitri, Damayanti and Sita* by Jamila Gavin, Methuen;
9. *The Story of Macbeth*, in *Shakespeare Stories* by Leon Garfield, Puffin;
10. *Mufaro's Beautiful Daughters* by John Steptoe, Puffin.

Encouraging reading and storytelling

These books were made available to the children, and the teachers read the opening few pages or arresting passages from some to whet the children's appetites and encourage them to read the complete story at home. This approach is a particularly effective device for the teacher to introduce children to new and exciting material, to widen their reading range and stir demand. On some occasions a complete short story such as *The Ceremony* by Martyn Copus was read to the children. Longer stories such as *The Great Leapfrog Contest* were serialised over several lessons. We agreed on the ways we would present the stories to the children:

*   Create the right environment, with the group of listeners sitting comfortably around the teacher in a half circle. Allow time and space for the children to enjoy and respond to the reading.
*   Deliver the text clearly and slowly in a voice which should be a little louder than normal conversation. Raise and lower the voice to gain effect. Avoid reading to the front row and make frequent eye-contact with the children.
*   Talk to the children about the story structure: introduction to the story, the setting of the scene, the development of the theme, the building up of characters and the conclusion.
*   Talk to the children about stylistic features: significant phrases, interesting details, choice of certain words, use of description and dialogue, repetition, sentence structure and figures of speech.
*   Demonstrate how – by using body language, gesture, pacing, intonation, pauses, expression, timing, tone of voice and accent – the atmosphere can be created and sustained.
*   Involve the Schools Library Service to mount a display of popular books, recommend stories and storytellers and help with reading sessions.

The story starters

Following our own presentations we were keen to encourage the pupils to tell and read some stories themselves. We used the 'guided reading' sessions for this. Working in groups of three and four, the children were given seven opening paragraphs and asked to place them in rank order. The more able children were given more demanding texts. The children were asked which of the openings they thought was the best, which the next, and so on. In the plenary session we discussed the characteristics of an effective opening, one which would capture the reader's attention, make him or her want to know happens next. We talked about how the stories might develop and how they might end. The groups were then asked to select one opening and complete the story which would be 'performed' to the whole class. They needed to:

- talk about how they thought the story would develop;
- plan out briefly the sequence of the story remembering to keep the theme simple;
- add interesting details and descriptions to maintain the atmosphere;
- develop the characters (maximum of four) saying what they thought they looked like and how they spoke and adding any other interesting details;
- write the story in draft form;
- follow the teacher's comments and suggestions and write the final draft;
- practise reading the story using different voices, tones, accents and facial expressions;
- use the prompt sheet to remind themselves of the sequence of events;
- perform or read the story.

The pupil presentations

For most pupils, sitting in front of a group of others, with all eyes upon them, is a stressful activity. We felt it vital that the young readers should be in an atmosphere of sympathetic interest. To reduce stress, we determined that some time should be spent on the pupils preparing for the reading, allowing them to gather and order the material, shape and clarify their ideas, rehearse the reading a few times, work on pace, pause, pitch, and practise reading the story onto a tape-recorder. Following the pupil readings, the class talked, in an atmosphere of good humour and encouragement, about the different presentations – which were really successful, how the readers created the tension, the sequence of the plots, the depiction of the characters and how the stories could be improved.

At the end of the project there had been noticeable gains in the quality of the oral and written work. The children had a wider knowledge of history, a more positive attitude to reading and a greater confidence in performing. In the course of hearing the stories read aloud, the children identified and assimilated some of the stylistic features typical of stories representing particular kinds of writing. For example, when James, aged 11, was writing an imaginary account of *The Gunpowder Plot*, he started with a powerful opening paragraph in which he set the scene and created an atmosphere of dark foreboding interwoven with his own fears of being caught:

Opening Paragraph: *Scene Setting*

There are echoing footsteps on the flagged floor above me. I hear rusty keys scraping in long forgotten locks, murmuring voices from some distant chamber, the slap, slap of water against the walls outside, distant shouts across the Thames, a dog barking. I hear every sound down here in the dark cellars, each one like a warning. The air is damp and the floor wet and slimy and reeking of the river.

Is the powder dry? Will the fuse carry the flame to the barrels? Are these walls too thick for the explosion to bring them crashing down? Will they discover me?

Simone began her story with a detailed character description.

Opening Paragraph: *Character Description*

Mr. Bowser had wild woolly hair, thick ginger eyebrows and a pale freckled face. He peered at Year 6 from behind great round tortoiseshell glasses and smiled so widely that he looked like a larger version of the frog in the tank on the display table. He wore a bright green jacket and yellow shirt which made him look even more frog-like. When he opened his mouth we all expected to hear a deep, frog-like croak.

Carla decided to start her story with a piece of lively dialogue.

Opening Paragraph: *Dialogue*

'I didn't say you couldn't come!' snapped Leane.
'Well, you never asked me,' said Lorna screwing up her mouth. 'And you never told me you were going.'
'I don't have to tell you everything, you know,' replied her supposed friend. 'And anyway you always complain when we go into town. You're just no fun these days.'
'I don't complain! I just don't want to spend all Saturday morning going from shop to shop. It's boring. There are a lot more interesting things to do.'
'Well, that's why I never told you we were going.' Leane looked in the mirror and flicked a strand of hair from her forehead. 'Anyway, Susie says you're no fun.'
'I thought it would be Susie!' exclaimed Lorna, screwing up her mouth.

John's opening paragraph takes us straight into the action.

Opening Paragraph: *Dramatic Opening*

Jason tugged and tugged at the rusty handle but the door would not budge.
'Help! Somebody! Help! I can't get out!' he shrieked. His voice echoed eerily around the empty room. It was getting dark now and shadows danced along the floor and it was getting cold. Jason shivered. He banged with a clenched fist on the door so hard his hand began to sting.
'Somebody! Help!' he cried. 'I'm locked in!'

Shared reading activities

I used one of my own stories with different Year 6, mixed-age, mixed-ability groups as a basis for in-depth study of a text.

Trouble at Blimpton Gap is an amusing story, written in very accessible language, with lively dialogue and some vivid description. Mrs Gabbitas takes her junior class on a study trip to Blimpton Gap on the east coast of Yorkshire. Her worst fears are realised when one of the pupils, Simon Morgan, gets his foot stuck in a rock just as the tide begins to turn.

I wanted to use this shared text to focus upon some key aspects of fiction writing:

- The Writer's Intention: 'Why did the author write this story?'
- The Genre: 'How can you tell that this is going to be an amusing school story?'
- Development of the Writing: Discussion of the writing process from the early idea, notes, first draft, subsequent drafts, proof reading to final published product.
- The Narrative Structure: Examination of how the text is structured with discussion of the beginning, the middle and the end.
- The Setting: How the writer attempts to paint a picture of the beach, the sea and cliffs using details and description.
- The Characters: How the writer attempts to create rounded, realistic believable characters.
- The Dialogue: How the writer attempts to create authentic conversations.
- The Language: The choice of words, phrases, significant detail, use of different sentence structures and use of punctuation.

Initially I dealt with the author's intention. It was explained to the children that texts are written for different reasons – to give information, persuade, amuse, entertain, frighten, challenge, provoke, warn – and they are organised in different ways – for example by narrating a story, describing an event, place or person or recreating a feeling as in a poem. The pupils were given the first two paragraphs and asked to try and guess what was the author's intention in writing this story and who was the intended audience. In *Trouble at Blimpton Gap* the story begins with a description of the teacher, the formidable Mrs Gabbitas:

Mrs Gabbitas would not have looked out of place behind the wet fish stall of the local outdoor market. A thick, brown woollen headscarf was wrapped round her head and tied in an enormous knot under her chin, and heavy green rubber boots appeared from beneath the old grey duffel coat which she always wore. She would not have sounded out of place behind the wet fish stall either. She had one of those unpleasantly deep loud voices often possessed by market traders.

Around Mrs Gabbitas, on a cold and windy afternoon, were a knot of pupils with icy hands and bored faces, listening to one of her all-too-familiar monologues. She had been going for ten minutes without seeming to draw breath.

Having established that this was an amusing story intended to entertain, we went on to discuss the different ways an author might begin a story. We decided that the five most often used story openings are:

- setting the scene;
- describing the central character;
- launching straight into the action;
- using dialogue;
- beginning with a question.

Trouble at Blimpton Gap opens with a description of the central character. The pupils, working in groups of five, were asked to rewrite the first few paragraphs of the story in the other four ways: with a description of the beach (setting), starting with Mrs Gabbitas's verbal exchanges with her pupils (dialogue), with a dramatic opening which takes the reader straight into the action and starting with a question. Here are four examples of what the pupils produced. There was a good degree of teacher intervention: words and phrases were discussed, dictionaries used, suggestions made and several drafts completed.

1. Blimpton Gap was a small area of curved grey sand backed by great looming black cliffs. The beach, pitted with shallow pools and outcrops of slimy seaweed-covered rocks, was not a favourite with holidaymakers who visited the larger, cleaner stretch of sand further down the coast. That afternoon, however, the usually deserted cove had visitors. Mrs Gabbitas stood facing her class giving them final instructions before they explored the coastline and completed their worksheets.

2. 'I hope everyone is listening!' boomed Mrs Gabbitas. 'Because I do not want to have to repeat myself.'
   Around the teacher on the cold, empty beach were her pupils with bored faces and icy hands.
   'Yes, Mrs Gabbitas,' they replied wearily.
   'Now we have the whole of the beach to ourselves this afternoon. Being cold and wet and windy and in the middle of November there is nobody else on the beach so we have it all to ourselves. I do not want anyone being silly. I want all of you to be sensible and spend the next hour finishing the worksheets. Now, on your right you will see the cliffs. Have a look.' Bored faces looked to the right. 'And on your left you will see the sea. Have a look.' Bored faces looked left. 'I do not want anyone up the cliffs or in the sea! Is that clear?'

'Yes, Mrs Gabbitas,' the children replied wearily.

3. "I'm stuck!' cried Simon.

'Stuck!' repeated Mrs Gabbitas, her voice echoing off the cliff. 'What do you mean, stuck? Get down here at once Simon Morgan!'

'I can't, Miss,' moaned the boy, clinging to the cliff side. 'I might fall off.'

'You are a silly boy, Simon Morgan,' said Mrs Gabbitas clambering over the slimy, seaweed-covered rocks to get to him. 'I said stay on the beach, not climb up the cliffs. I just knew this would happen.'

4. Why had the teacher decided to take her class to the coast on such a cold, wet, November afternoon when the wind whistled down the beach and cut into the children's faces like a knife? Why had she not waited until summer when the sun warms the sand and the sea glistens and the beach would have been full of holidaymakers? Why had she ignored the warnings printed for all to see and displayed on the large square sign on Marine Drive? No-one ever found out.

Having discussed how a story might begin we then turned our attention to how it might develop. During the reading we investigated the craft of the writer, considering plot, character, structure, language features, vocabulary, grammatical features and the technical aspects of punctuation and spelling. Further investigative work, which was carried out in groups and pairs, involved the children tackling some cloze procedure strategies, text transformation, substitution and deletion exercises.

An essential part of the Literacy Hour is the sensitive interrogation of a complete text, when the teacher explores with the whole class just how the writer creates a story, poem, play or factual account. With this story I wanted to:

• Share my own ideas about the text, e.g. 'At this point I wanted to slow down the pace so I interrupted the fast moving dialogue with a short description', 'Notice the way I have used short sentences to quicken up the pace in this part the story', 'The story ends very quickly after the boy is rescued because to have continued writing would have resulted in an anticlimax.'

• Encourage the children to give their opinions, e.g. 'How would you have felt if you had been Royston?' 'What do you think I meant in this sentence?' 'Can you explain why Mrs Gabbitas decides to do this?' 'Describe Penelope Pringle,' 'What sort of boy is Ravjir Singh?'

• Challenge the children to justify their points of view by reference to the text, e.g. 'How do you know Simon was afraid?' 'Where are the clues in the story which tell us how it might end?' 'Could the story have ended in a different way?' 'When in the story, do you think, did Mrs Gabbitas realise the seriousness of the situation?' 'Are Royston's suggestions helpful?' 'What sort of teacher is Mrs Gabbitas?' 'What was Mrs Gabbitas's reaction to the comments of the bus driver at the end?.'

• Avoid fierce interrogation or lectures – appreciation of the story comes before analysis.

• Value each contribution, e.g. 'That's a good point', 'It's interesting you should say that . . .'

• Use specialist terminology (meta-language) to provide the language for talking about the text, e.g. 'Would anyone like to comment on the use the writer makes of adjectives?' 'Why do I start this sentence with an adverb?' 'Why is an exclamation mark used here?'

In one session we analysed two sections of the story in some detail. These extracts describe the key moments in the story and are good examples of the building up of suspense. They also lead on naturally to writing activities.

Mrs Gabbitas, summoned by Ravjir Singh, has arrived at the black rocks to find Simon Morgan, his face red with exertion, attempting to pull his foot out of a deep cleft. Despite her efforts, she cannot free him and she becomes all-too-aware that the tide is coming in at an alarming rate.

> For once in her life Mrs Gabbitas was silent, completely lost for words.
> Through her mind rushed the most terrifying thoughts: the cold North Sea rushing relentlessly across the beach, sweeping over the rocks, and swallowing up the trapped child.
> 'Miss, Miss!' pestered Royston. 'I could cut the bottom off my lemonade bottle and Simon could use it as a kind of breathing tube when the sea goes over his head.'
> 'Miss, Miss!' There came a strangled cry from Simon.
> 'Royston,' Mrs Gabbitas spoke through gritted teeth, 'will you be quiet. There's no question of the sea going over Simon's head. We'll soon have him out of there. Now you and Ravjir run up to the road and stop the first car you see. Tell the driver to get help.'
> The two boys scurried off.
> 'And be careful!' she shouted after them.

Mrs Gabbitas despatches several more pupils to get help but they all return, ten minutes later, to tell her that they have had no success.

> The sea was now swirling around Simon's knees and tipping him off balance. He was quiet, white and trembling. The rest of the children watched anxiously from the sand. Mrs Gabbitas, with water now over her boots, gripped his hand tightly and prayed. Royston scrambled over the slippery rocks towards her, his voice ringing loudly.
> 'Miss, Miss!' he cried. 'Nobody would stop. They thought we were messing about. They wouldn't stop!'

In groups, the children were asked to read the extracts and, guided by a series of questions I had provided, consider a number of things. They were asked to make notes on paper and be prepared to share their opinions with the whole group in the plenary session later on. Their tasks included discussing and noting down how the writer creates suspense, picking out the verbs which emphasise fast action, investigating synonyms for some of the nouns and adjectives, explaining what effects words like 'strangled', 'relentlessly', 'gritted', 'scurried' create in their minds, examining and commenting upon the use of different sentence structures and items of punctuation.

Two sessions were devoted to examining how a writer uses description in a story. The children were asked to look at three pieces of text (unrelated to *Trouble at Blimpton Gap*) and examine how the different writers use adjectives, significant detail and descriptive phrases to paint a picture of the place in words.

1. Entering the oily darkness of the garage was like walking into the jaws of some great metal-eating creature. It was a tangled mass of pipes, plugs, coils, drums, cans, wires and broken machines, a jungle of junk. Behind a mound of crumpled paint tins, crusted with rust, were cardboard boxes bursting with jars and pots and glass bottles. An old pine cupboard with missing doors leaned against a wall and a pile of worn tyres teetered like a black tower about to collapse. On the shelves spanners, screwdrivers, hammers, pliers, chisels, clamps, shears and all manner of tools were heaped haphazardly. Somewhere in the middle of all this was the box.

2. The allotment stretched down the side of the canal, along the other bank. Neat patches of hard, dark brown earth were full of cabbages, sprouts and bright green leeks. There were old windowless sheds, weathered and worn, bean rows and empty trellises, cold frames littered with splintered glass, broken fencing and piles of vegetable refuse.

    Adolph's allotment was different from all the surrounding plots. A row of carefully-pruned bushes lined a narrow cinder path which led to a copse of fruit trees, laden with apples and pears. The rows of sprouts stood up straight and solid like ranks of soldiers and the mounds of soil covering the potatoes were heaped carefully. There was not a weed in sight. Everything was so tidy and ordered. A brightly-painted green shed stood in the corner of the plot and on the roof a small wooden figure moved in the wind as if digging.

    'He's not here,' said Parky smiling.

3. The door creaked open and he entered the musty darkness of the attic – the forbidden room. Dominic squeezed up his eyes in the half light and peered at the scene before him. It was an Aladdin's cave of untold riches, a storehouse of fascinating objects and hidden treasures. He crept like a burglar between the old ladder-backed chairs and dusty cupboards, clambered over rolls of carpet, squeezed between carefully-stacked boxes full of cracked teapots, twisted brass candlesticks, books bound in red leather, chipped vases and tarnished cutlery. An old black typewriter with broken keys sat on a bamboo table, next to an old-fashioned telephone with twisted brown flex and a silver dialling ring. He lifted the telephone carefully, almost expecting to hear the dialling tone. He turned when he heard the wind in the trees outside and the attic door creak. Dominic watched helplessly as the heavy door clicked shut. He was locked in.

The children were then given two very pedestrian pieces and asked to put in adjectives and adverbs to make the description more interesting and vivid, change some of the words to give greater impact, use connectives to extend the sentences and use detail to 'embroider' the texts:

1. The hospital was a big building. Behind the big doors was a reception area. A woman sat at a desk writing. Lots of corridors went in different directions and there were signs on the wall saying which department was where and how to get to them. Rows of people waited to be seen to. There were doctors in white coats and nurses in uniform and porters in grey overalls.

2. The wood was very dark. Tall trees were everywhere and lots of bushes grew along the path. The path was narrow and went through the centre of the wood. It

had rained the night before so everything was wet. The path was now quite muddy. There were some colourful flowers growing on the banks. I could hear the little stream gurgling away. I could hear the sounds of the birds singing in the trees.

Using *Trouble at Blimpton Gap* with a third class of Year 6 children, I focused specifically on the writer's use of grammar and punctuation. The 'shared reading' session was used for close reading, discussion of tense, spellings and parts of speech and for helping the children to identify other features of grammar and punctuation and for encouraging them to talk about functions and effects. In the group work I asked them to read an extract from the story and transform it from the past into the present tense and then from third person to first person. The pupils were then given eight sentences and asked to circle any verbs that they felt could be made more precise or expressive and provide alternatives. They were asked to put in adjectives and adverbs to make the sentences more interesting, change some of the words to give greater impact, use connectives to extend the sentences and write out the different ways the sentences could be structured.

1. Mrs Gabbitas got on the coach.
2. Ravjir looked at the sea.
3. Royston stood beneath the cliffs.
4. Penelope was wearing a coat, scarf, hat and gloves.
5. Timothy Joseph picked up a piece of driftwood from the beach.
6. Simon had got his foot stuck in the rocks.
7. 'Go and get help,' said Mrs Gabbitas.
8. Mrs Gabbitas fell in the sea.

Having studied and discussed the opening and the development of the story with another Year 6 group, we turned our attention to the conclusion. *Trouble at Blimpton Gap* is in the genre of an amusing school adventure story and therefore has to conclude on a happy note. Simon, try as he might, just cannot free his foot from the deep cleft in the rock. Mrs Gabbitas sends two children to the holiday cottages at the end of the beach to get help. She despatches a further two pupils to the telephone kiosk on Marine Drive with the instruction to ring the police. Royston and Ravjir are sent to stop a car and get help. The children return with direful news: the holiday cottages are all locked up, the telephone kiosk has been vandalised and to Simon's horror, he sees Royston running across the sands with no helpful driver.

We considered the various alternatives and a lively discussion followed. There was, of course, the old favourite – 'I woke up and it was only a dream' – which we discounted. One group ended the story where Simon managed to pull his foot out just as the water reached his neck. This gave me an excellent opportunity to talk about tension and suspense in stories. Another group described a chaotic scene where ambulance, air sea rescue, lifeboat, police cars and fire engines all converge on the trapped child who manages to pull his foot out at the very moment when they reach him. Mrs Gabbitas, red-faced and inarticulate, has to explain to an angry policeman that the rescue services were not needed after all. One group suggested a 'twist' to the tale. When all the police, lifeboat, fire and ambulance crews have departed, Simon announces, in a frail little voice, that he has got his foot stuck again.

Sensitive interrogation of stories helps children focus upon the criteria for successful writing. At the end of the week we recapped the issues discussed earlier: character through action and description, powerful vocabulary, sentence length, paragraphing, use of dialogue, significant detail, an understanding of what constitutes good quality writing.

The same story formed the basis for a range of drama activities:

- *Improvisation:* Different groups acted out five parts of the story and brought the text to life through characterisation, interaction, mime and movement;
    1. the scene on the beach at the very beginning;
    2. the telling off of Royston by the teacher;
    3. when Simon tried to pull his foot out of the rock;
    4. the teacher's instruction to the pupils to get help;
    5. the arrival of the coach at the end.

Following the acting-out the children were asked to comment on the improvisation and evaluate the work of the other groups.

- *Tableaux:* Small groups worked to produce frozen moments or 'stills' in the story. Children using facial expressions and body posture recreated key moments:
    1. the children listening to the teacher's instructions;
    2. Penelope telling Mrs Gabbitas about Royston's misbehaviour;
    3. Ravjir telling Mrs Gabbitas about Simon stuck in the rocks;
    4. the teacher's arrival at the rocks to find the trapped boy;
    5. the teacher's reaction on hearing that the tide is coming in;
    6. the arrival of the coach at the end.

- *Hot Seating:* Different characters from the story were brought to life by the children who assumed certain roles and were interrogated by the class. Questions began on a simple level about who they were, where they lived, their family, friends, things they liked to do, and moved into more searching questions about their actions, feelings and motives.

The work based upon the short story *Trouble at Blimpton Gap* led naturally into a range of 'shared' and 'guided' reading and writing activities. The children were organised into groups and set different tasks which included:

- Write Mrs Gabbitas's letter to parents with details about the proposed trip to Blimpton Gap.
- Write a short newspaper article with the headline 'BOY TRAPPED IN ROCKS!' which tells the story of Simon's ordeal.
- Dramatise the part in the story where the children tell Mrs Gabbitas that help is not coming.
- Write a diary entry from the point of view of: Mrs Gabbitas, Ravjir Singh or Simon Morgan.
- Compile a small file of correspondence relating to the story: a letter of complaint from Simon's mother, a memorandum from the head teacher asking Mrs Gabbitas for an explanation, a letter from a reader of the newspaper in which an article about the incident occurred.
- Write a continuation of the story – what happens on the Monday morning back at school?

- Write a short interview in the form of a dialogue between: the head teacher and Mrs Gabbitas, the head teacher and Simon Morgan, the head teacher and Simon's father or the bus driver and Mrs Gabbitas.
- Devise a comic strip. The story should be told in eight frames with speech or thought bubbles and short pieces of narrative.
- Write a monologue, which could be in the form of telephone conversation, from the point of view of Mrs Gabbitas, Simon Morgan or the head teacher.
- Write a story on a similar theme: 'Trapped!'
- Write Royston's school report from Mrs Gabbitas.
- The story is to be adapted for television. Write the Casting Director's notes on the main characters describing: what they wear, what they look like and how they speak.
- Write a booklet called 'Safety First' with some advice for teachers taking children on school trips.

Guided reading activities

'Shared reading' activities, such as the ones described above, lead naturally into the 'guided reading' of a whole range of other material. Here the teacher supports small groups of children with multiple copies of a text matched to the children's independent reading level. The texts described in Part I are suitable for guided reading. They are appealing, sufficiently challenging, produced in an appropriate print size and of manageable length. The aim of the guided reading sessions is to:

- Develop the ideas raised in the shared reading sessions, e.g. 'What sort of genre does this story fall into?' 'How does the story begin – with setting, character description, action or dialogue?' 'Can you predict what will happen next?' 'How do you think she will react when she hears the news?'
- Investigate the author's point of view, e.g. 'Why does the author mention this character at this point?' 'Is this part of the story intended to shock the reader?'
- Analyse character, e.g. 'Why did he say this?' 'What was she thinking at this point?' 'Did the reaction of this character surprise you?.'
- Present the story using different voices, tones, accents and facial expressions.
- Give a personal response to the text, e.g. 'Would you like this person as a friend?' 'Would you have done what he did?' 'How do you imagine she feels when she hears the news?'
- Develop independent reading strategies by listening to children read the text.
- Examine the language, using specialist terminology.
- Discuss the cover design and the blurb on the back of the book.
- Undertake a range of writing activities based on the text.
- Undertake a range of drama activities related to the text.

It is often useful in the guided reading sessions to organise the children into ability groups and give different texts varying in degree of difficulty. Each child reads the entire story independently and might, on occasions, be given a Story Summary Sheet to record what has been read. The Story Summary Sheet is useful to assess the children's understanding and reinforce the work that has been undertaken in the shared reading sessions on plot and story structure. Clearly such a sheet would not be used on every occasion that a child reads a book in the guided reading sessions. Were that to be the case the children would soon be turned off reading.

STORY SUMMARY SHEET

- Name of reader: ....
- Title of the story: ....
- Author of the story: ....
- Date read: ....
- The story begins when:

- The first thing that happens is:

- After that:

- And then:

- The story ends when:

- Personal comment:

The guided reading session gives the teacher the opportunity of spending some time with each group talking about the text, listening to the children read and helping them with particular difficulties they might encounter. Following the quiet reading, the groups might be asked to investigate the texts. It is important to stress that guided reading is not just reading in unison round the group or silent individual reading or for the teacher to merely 'hear readers'. It is far more than this. It is a time when the children deepen and widen their understanding of the text, learn how to use aspects of language, engage in reading strategies such as prediction and self-correction and learn the skills and strategies to read increasingly difficult material. To keep them on task, the teacher might, on occasions, give each group a series of prompts:

PROMP SHEET FOR GUIDED READING

- Title of the Story
  What does the title make you think the story will be about?
- Author of the story
  Have you read any other stories by this author?
  What are the themes he or she usually writes about?
  Is this story different?
- Introduction
  Read the first few paragraphs.
  Does the opening begin with: scene setting, character description, dialogue or does it take the reader straight into the action?
  Does it begin in another way?
- Characters
  Identify the main characters in this story.
  What are they like?
  What are the most important events which happen to the characters?
  What are the main difficulties the characters have to overcome?
- Development
  How does the writer keep the reader's interest?
  Did you think the story would continue in the way it did?
- Conclusion
  Did you expect the story to end as it did?
  Did the opening of the story prepare you for the ending?
- Language
  Are there any descriptions, phrases, words which stood out?
  Are there any parts of the story you could not understand?
- Personal Comment
  What is your opinion of this story?
  Would you like to read another story by this author?

The guided reading session can be followed by a plenary when the stories are discussed. Finally the children might be allowed to select stories to read on their own without any assistance ('independent reading'). This is an opportunity for them to apply and develop the skills they have learned in shared and guided reading, practise and extend their reading skills, select books they are interested in and read at their own pace. A time should be set aside each day for independent reading and from their very first week in school children should get into the habit of selecting books which appeal to them and sitting quietly to read. The various stories, poetry anthologies and non-fiction material described earlier offer a rich range suitable for independent reading.

Chapter 6

Encouraging an Appreciation of Poetry

For many, poetry is dinned into their unwilling heads at school, trailed across their noses in restless adolescence and ever after considered part of another world. Not the real, ordinary world.

(Bragg 1983)

Poetry is accorded an important place in the National Curriculum and in the National Literacy Strategy. Teachers are charged with introducing to all their pupils the great range of verse, encouraging them to enjoy and appreciate the rhymes and rhythms of the language and learn the skills to write good quality poems themselves. Children are entitled, from the very earliest age, to hear and study a range of material which is rich and varied: funny, exciting, spooky, vigorous, fresh, playful, reflective verse, poems of intensity and excitement, where the language is crisp, clear and forceful and rhymes full of pleasures and surprises.

The teacher might heighten children's awareness of poetry by using a range of strategies. These could include:

1. Read a wide selection of poems to children over the year. For example you might start the day with a poem – not to be discussed or analysed, just to be enjoyed. There does not always have to be follow-on work. Simply reading poetry to children 'beds their ear' with the richest kind of language.
2. Compile a list of poems suitable for different age groups and make a collection of poetry posters and cards.
3. Invite poets into school to work with the children and share their experiences of the process of writing: where ideas come from, the research they have to undertake, how they draft and revise, proof read and submit for publication. Listening to poets like Michael Rosen, Peter Dixon, Irene Rawnsley, Kit Wright, Brian Moses, June Crebbin and Berlie Doherty reading and interpreting their own work, will fascinate and inspire children. The poet's visit might be arranged as part of a Book Week or Literature Festival and the local Arts Group, a publisher or The Poetry Society, 22 Betterton Street, London, WC2H 9BU, will be able to advise and may be able to help with funding.
4. Display a wide selection of material and ask the children to browse and then from an anthology select just one short verse, perhaps a limerick or a haiku. Ask each child to copy out the selected poem and decorate it, commit it to memory and

then recite it to the others in the class. A collection of these short poems could be put together into a poetry booklet or form part of a colourful display.

5. Mount displays of poetry anthologies, book jackets and posters in school corridors and classrooms. Publishers will often provide material.

6. Organise an evening for teachers, parents, governors and children when a speaker such as an author, adviser or member of The School Library Service talks about the importance of poetry. As part of the event the children could be asked to read or perform a selection of poems (including their own) accompanied by music and mime. This could include a dramatic reading or a group choral presentation.

7. Spend a little time each week reading and discussing a longer more demanding poem. When studying a poem in the Literacy Hour do so sensitively. Appreciation comes before analysis.

8. Enlarge short poems and hang them from the ceilings or decorate classrooms and corridors with them. The range of colourful and varied pictorial charts and poetry posters produced by The Poetry Society will brighten up any classroom or corridor and raise the profile of poetry in school and can be used for shared reading activities in the Literacy Hour.

9. If you have a computer in the classroom leave it on with a poem screen saver.

10. Integrate poetry into the topic work you undertake. The Saison Poetry Library produces an excellent range of Poetry Packs which contain worksheets based on themes: *Food, Animals, Places, Traditions, Light and Dark, Friends and Enemies, Magic and Mystery.*

Chapter 7
Responding to Poetry at Key Stage 1

There is no doubt that the combination of rhythm, rhyme and striking illustration brings the reader the closest to a successful and satisfying reading that he or she has ever known. The lines unfold effortlessly once the text has been heard once or twice and the new reader experiences a flow and fluency that may hitherto have been elusive. Then the reader is liberated to enjoy poetry's particular way of saying things.

(Graham and Placket 1982)

When they arrive at nursery, many children will have already had some experience of poetry. They will have heard television jingles, pop songs, nursery rhymes and snippets of verse. Some will be familiar with the traditional rhymes and rhythms of such favourites as:

Round and round the garden,
Like a Teddy Bear;
One step, two step,
Tickle under there!

Ring a ring o'roses,
A pocket full of posies,
A-tishoo, a-tishoo,
We all fall down.

At playgroup they may have been introduced to the lively rhythms, strong rhymes, choruses and repetitions of modern as well as traditional material, encouraged to join in and enjoy the verse. Sometimes children are introduced to old and unusual rhymes, and told about the old fashioned words and expressions:

A farmer was trotting
Upon his grey mare,
Bumpety, Bumpety, Bump!
With his daughter behind him,
So rosy and fair,
Lumpety, Lumpety, Lump!

A raven cried 'Croak!'
And they all tumbled down.
Bumpety, Bumpety, Bump!
The mare broke her knees,
And the farmer his crown,
Lumpety, Lumpety, Lump!

The mischievous raven
Flew laughing away,
Bumpety, Bumpety, Bump!
And he vowed he would serve them
The same the next day,
Lumpety, Lumpety, Lump!

The infant teacher draws on this early experience and encourages the children to perform the little rhymes they know: *Humpty Dumpty, Miss Molly had a Dolly, Georgie Porgy, Simple Simon, Jack and Jill, The Grand Old Duke of York* and *Mary, Mary, Quite Contrary*. She continues to read to the children regularly, encouraging them to sound out the words, hear the rhymes and clap to the rhythms.

Not last night, but the night before,
Twenty four robbers came a-knocking at my door.
I asked them what they wanted,
And this is what they said:
'H...O...T...HOT PEPPERS!'

She presents a wide range of verse, which relates to what children see and hear around them, stimulating their imaginations, enriching their vocabulary and building listening skills. She introduces them to some new and inventive poems full of engaging humour and lively language. She delights them with poems about mummies and daddies, big sisters and baby brothers, snowflakes and sunshine, sand and sea, caterpillars and cats, toy soldiers and teddy bears:

Teddy Bear, Teddy Bear,
Go upstairs.
Teddy Bear, Teddy Bear,
Say your prayers.
Teddy Bear, Teddy Bear,
Turn out the light.
Teddy Bear, Teddy Bear,
Say, 'Good night.'

On some occasions she will present a poem dramatically, starting in a hushed whisper and increasing the volume and the pace to bring the verse to dramatic conclusion:

In a dark, dark wood
There is a dark, dark house
And in that dark, dark house
There is a dark, dark hall,

And that dark, dark hall
Leads to a dark, dark door,
And behind that dark, dark door
There is a dark, dark room,
And in that dark, dark room
There is a dark, dark curtain,
And behind the dark, dark curtain
There is a dark, dark cupboard,
And in that dark, dark cupboard
There is a dark, dark shelf,
And on that dark, dark shelf
There is a dark, dark box,
And in that dark, dark box
There is a ... MOUSE!

The infant teacher sometimes challenges the children to think about the poems she reads to them, share their ideas and answer questions, identify letters and words and solve language riddles.

Who am I?
Whisky, frisky, hippity hop,
Up I climb to the very top!
Whirly, twirly round and round,
Down I scamper to the ground.
Hurly, curly, what a tail,
Tall as a feather, broad as a sail.
Where's my supper? In the shell.
Snappity, crackity, out it fell.

In these early stage the teacher aims to:

- encourage the children to listen attentively to the rhythm and rhymes of poetry;
- make poems important and enjoyable for them;
- use their knowledge of alphabet letters and simple words;
- encourage them to actively participate in the reading when they feel confident to do so;
- stimulate their own spoken language, encouraging them to speak with clarity, confidence and expression;
- teach them about some of the surface features of writing such as spelling and punctuation, stressing high frequency words like *said, see, make, made, come, because, him, her, when, where, with, will, look;*
- help them understand how successful poems work;
- learn the terminology of poetry: rhyme, rhythm, theme;
- foster their voluntary independent reading of poems.

The selection of poems which follow includes a range of traditional verse forms and some of my own poems. All can be copied by teachers for use with children. Ideas for presenting them are offered and some starting points and strategies to encourage young children to write their own poems.

In the early years children should be encouraged to join in with the performance of the poems. Much of the verse presented to young children will have strong rhymes and lively rhythms and children will delight in clapping their hands, clicking their fingers and using their voices. Initially the teacher might read the verse a couple of times to reveal the poem's qualities such as the sounds, rhyming words, beat, cadences, language patterns and repetitions. Many of the traditional and well loved rhymes are ideal for this and children can invent additional verses and extra actions:

> Here we go round the mulberry bush,
> The mulberry bush, the mulberry bush,
> Here we go round the mulberry bush
> On a cold and frosty morning.
>
> This is the way we wash ourselves,
> Wash ourselves, wash ourselves,
> This is the way we wash ourselves
> On a cold and frosty morning.
>
> This is the way we brush our teeth,
> Brush our teeth, brush our teeth,
> This is the way we brush our teeth
> On a cold and frosty morning.
>
> This is the way we put on our clothes,
> Put on our clothes, put on our clothes,
> This is the way we put on our clothes
> On a cold and frosty morning.
>
> This is the way we comb our hair,
> Comb our hair, comb our hair,
> This is the way we comb our hair
> On a cold and frosty morning.
>
> This is the way we clean our shoes,
> Clean our shoes, clean our shoes,
> This is the way we clean our shoes
> On a cold and frosty morning.

In the Literacy Hour young children should experience a whole range of verse: nursery rhymes, playground chants, simple counting rhymes, action verse, simple syllabic poetry, songs and lyrics, patterned poems and rhyming couplets.

With one group of infants I explored the sounds and spellings of the children's names before looking together at one of my own poems. We then tried to find rhymes for the names of children in the class and write some rhyming couplets based upon them.

Rhyme-Time
Our teacher, Mrs Paradigm,
To teach us children how to rhyme,

Has asked us all to take our name
And find a word that sounds the same.
And so we did.
Kim is slim,
Dean's a dream,
Brenda is tender and
Sally is pally.
Trevor is clever,
Kate is great,
Jean is lean but
Rowena is leaner.
Scott is hot,
Andy is dandy,
Rick is slick and
Wendy is trendy.
Terry is merry,
Bill is brill',
Pete is sweet but
Rita is sweeter.
Dwight is bright,
Roisin is clean,
Dave is brave and
Molly is jolly.
Paul is tall,
Bhupa is super,
Dean is keen but
Gina is keener.
Mabel is able,
Kitty is pretty,
Grace is ace and
Cecil is special.
Nancy is fancy,
Mick is quick,
Luke is cute but
Danuta is cuter.
Pip is hip,
Clare is fair,
Danny is canny and
Liz is a whizz.
The trouble is my name is Matt,
And I can't think of a rhyme for that!
(Well, not a nice one anyway).

The children were then asked to provide suitable words for the spaces in the following two poems. The original poem is printed alongside.

Today I Feel

Today, I feel:	Today, I feel:
Pleased as Punch	Pleased as Punch
Fit as a fiddle	Fit as a fiddle
Keen as a knife	Keen as a knife
Hot as a griddle	Hot as a griddle
Bold as brass	Bold as brass
Bouncy as a ………..	Bouncy as a ball
Keen as mustard	Keen as mustard
High as a …………...	High as a wall
Bright as a button	Bright as a button
Fragrant as heather	Fragrant as heather
Fresh as a daisy	Fresh as a daisy
Light as a …………...	Light as a feather
Chirpy as a cricket	Chirpy as a cricket
Sound as a bell	Sound as a bell
Sharp as a …………...	Sharp as a needle
Deep as a …………...	Deep as a well
High as a …………...	High as a kite
Strong as a …………...	Strong as a bull
Bubbly as bath water	Bubbly as bath water
Warm as ……………..	Warm as wool
Clean as a new pin	Clean as a new pin
Shiny as money	Shiny as money
Quick as …………...	Quick as lightning
Sweet as …………...	Sweet as honey
Cool as a cucumber	Cool as a cucumber
Fast as a …………...	Fast as a hare
Right as …………...	Right as rain
Brave as a …………...	Brave as a bear
Lively as a monkey	Lively as a monkey
Busy as a …………...	Busy as a bee
Good as …………...	Good as gold
Free as the ………….	Free as the sea

I'm so happy – I'm just lost for words!

House Noises

Doors ………………...	Doors bang
Toilet ………………...	Toilet flushes
Washer ……………….	Washer hums
Shower ……………….	Shower gushes
Taps ………………….	Taps drip
Fire …………………...	Fire crackles
Curtains ……………...	Curtains rustle
Dishes ………………...	Dishes rattle
Doorbell ……………...	Doorbell buzzes
Stairs ………………...	Stairs creak

Telephone	Telephone rings
Cupboards	Cupboards squeak
Chairs	Chairs scrape
Clocks	Clocks chime
I couldn't find another rhyme.	I couldn't find another rhyme.

In the anthologies recommended earlier are many short poems, like the ones below, which children might be encouraged to copy out, illustrate and learn:

> Rain on the green grass,
> And rain on the tree,
> Rain on the housetop,
> But don't rain on me!

> There's music in the hammer,
> There's music in the nail
> There's music in the pussy cat
> When you tread on her tail!

> My father owns the butcher shop,
> My mother cuts the meat,
> And I'm the little hot dog,
> That runs around the street.

> In August, when the days are hot,
> I like to find a shady spot,
> I hardly move a single bit,
> And sit,
>   And sit,
>   And sit,
>   And sit.

Many poems for young children are simple in structure, rhythmic, repetitive but have particular qualities which appeal and encourage a lively response. The following poem was read twice to the children before they joined in using their fingers and eyes.

> I have ten little fingers
> And they all belong to me.
> I can make them do things.
> Would you like to see?
> I can shut them up tight,
> Or open them wide.
> I can put them together,
> Or make them all hide.
> I can make then jump up high,
> I can make them jump down low,
> I can fold them quietly,
> And hold them just so.

A discussion followed in which the children were asked to talk about their fingers: size, colour, shape, skin texture and shape of the nails, and key words were put on the board. Other poems about hands and fingers were then presented and children asked to mime various actions as we read the poems together. These poems included:

- *Incy Wincy Spider* (traditional);
- *One, Two, Three, Four, Five* in *The Way the Wind Blows*, compiled by Leonard Clark, Evans;
- *Fingers and Toes*, two delightful poems by Shirley Hughes in *Rhymes for Annie Rose* by Shirley Hughes, Bodley Head;
- *Chip Chop* in *This Little Puffin*, compiled by Elizabeth Metterson, Puffin;
- *Knock at the Door* in *A Day of Rhymes*, selected by Sarah Pooley, Red Fox;
- *Holding Hands* by Eleanor M. Linkin in *The Walker Book of Read-Aloud Rhymes for the Very Young*, selected by Jack Prelutsky, Walker Books.

To stimulate the children's own spoken language and encourage them to speak with clarity and confidence, I selected a range of poems to develop in them an 'ear for language' and teach them about the importance of timing, pace, expression, tone of voice, accent and intonation:

Five Little Owls
Five little owls in an old oak tree,
Fluffy and puffy as owls should be,
Blinking and winking with big round eyes
At the big round moon that hung in the sky.
As it passed high above, I could hear one say,
'There'll be mouse for supper for us owls today!'
Then all of them hooted, 'To-whit, To-whoo!
Yes, mouse for supper, Hoo-hoo, Hoo-hoo!'

Down in the Long Grass
Down in the long grass,
Coiled in a heap,
Lies a fat, flat snake
And he's fast asleep.
When he hears you coming
And he sees the grasses blow
He slithers and he slides
And he moves to and fro,
Up and down,
And in and out,
Watch him slowly move about.
See his jaws are open so –
'Ouch!' he's caught my finger! Oh!'

Time for Bed
The evening is coming,
The sun sinks to rest,

The birds are all flying
Straight home to their nests.
'Caw! Caw!' cries the crow,
As he flies overhead,
It's time little children, we're going to bed.

Here comes the pony,
His work is all done.
Down through the meadow,
He takes a good run.
Clipperty-clop go his hooves,
And down goes his head,
It's time little children, we're going to bed.

Here comes the farmer,
He's called it a day.
He's finished his reaping,
And bundled the hay.
He sighs at the sky,
And the sunset so red,
It's time little children, we're going to bed.

It's a Crow's Life
Nobody loves me . . . . Aaaaaaaaah.
Everybody hates me . . . . Aaaaaaaaah.
I think I'll eat some worms . . . . Uuuuuuuugh!

Big, fat squelchy ones,
Long, thin skinny ones,
Small, baby squirmy ones.
There's nothing more tasty that a wiggly worm.
Bite off their heads,
Schlurp! Schlurp! Yum, Yum,
Throw away their tails.
There's nothing more tasty than a worm in your tum!

I'm only a small little bird, but soon I'll grow
On worms three times a day.
You ought to try them for yourself
Served up on a tray.

Nobody loves me . . . . Aaaaaaaaah.
Everybody hates me . . . . Aaaaaaaaah.
I think I'll eat some worms . . . . Uuuuuuuugh!

The Hairy Toe
There was once an old woman,
Who found a hairy toe.
She took it home with her,
And by the fireside glow,

She stared at it and stared at it,
And heard the cold winds blow:

Who's got my Hair-r-r-r-y To-o-o-o-e?
Who's got my Hair-r-r-r-y To-o-o-o-e?

That night when it was dark and cold,
She clambered into bed,
And blew the spluttering candle out,
And a voice came in her head:

Who's got my Hair-r-r-r-y To-o-o-o-e?
Who's got my Hair-r-r-r-y To-o-o-o-e?

She heard a creaking on the stairs,
She heard the floorboard groan,
She heard the rattling windows cry
She heard the rafters moan:

Who's got my Hair-r-r-r-y To-o-o-o-e?
Who's got my Hair-r-r-r-y To-o-o-o-e?

Then something slipped in through the door,
And crept towards her bed,
And as shadows danced across the walls,
She heard a voice which said:

Who's got my Hair-r-r-r-y To-o-o-o-e?
Who's got my Hair-r-r-r-y To-o-o-o-e?

'I've got it!' said the woman,
'But don't want it any more.
You'll find it on the table
Behind the kitchen door.'

Then she snuggled 'neath the blankets,
As she had done before,
And heard a voice a-singing across the distant moor:

I've got my Hair-r-r-r-y To-o-o-o-e!
I've got my Hair-r-r-r-y To-o-o-o-e!

Finally longer and more complex poems were read and discussed. The children were encouraged to listen attentively to the rhythm and rhymes of the verse, actively participate in the reading when they felt confident in doing so, identify high frequency words, consider the punctuation, use of adjectives and direct speech and discuss the imagery and repetition. But all this was done after they had heard the poems read several times and enjoyed them. Here is one of my own poems:

Auntie Penny's Pets
Auntie Penny has a parrot,
She calls him Captain Jack.

He has red and yellow feathers
And a beak of shiny black.
He has eyes like tiny pebbles,
And claws of scaly grey,
And he squawks and talks,
And talks and squawks,
All the livelong day.

Auntie Penny has a Scotty dog,
She calls him Mr. Mac.
He has little legs and a stumpy tail,
And a very hairy back.
He has teeth as sharp as icicles,
And eyes like diamonds bright,
And he snaps and yaps,
And yaps and snaps,
Morning, noon and night.

Auntie Penny has a Siamese cat,
She calls her The Old Maid.
She has silver fur as soft as silk,
And eyes of polished jade.
She has pointed claws as sharp as knives,
And whiskers thin as wire,
And she purrs and purrs,
And never stirs,
Curled up by the fire.

Auntie Penny has a donkey,
She calls him Irish Brian.
He is small and thin and bony,
With hooves as hard as iron.
He has teeth as square as tombstones,
And a mane as red as rust,
And he neighs and brays,
And brays and neighs,
From daylight until dusk.

Auntie Penny has a portly pig,
She calls her Mrs Stout.
She is round and fat and bristly,
With a wet and wiggly snout.
She has a curly tail like a coiled-up spring,
And a coat of purest white,
And she grunts and digs,
With the other pigs,
From daybreak until night.

Auntie Penny has a husband,
His name is Uncle Paul.
He's very, very quiet,
In fact, he hardly speaks at all.
He cooks and cleans and washes,
And tidies all the house,
And he tiptoes round,
Without a sound,
As quiet as a mouse.

Auntie Penny, she likes all her pets:
The Old Maid and Captain Jack,
Mrs Stout and Irish Brian,
And grumpy Mr. Mac,
But she has a special favourite,
He's the quietest of them all,
And she loves him best,
More than all the rest,
And his name is Uncle Paul.

Six Little Chicks
Said the first little chicken,
With a strange little squirm,
'I wish that I could find myself,
A fat juicy worm.'

Said the second little chicken,
With an odd little shrug,
'I wish that I could find myself,
A fat tasty slug.'

Said the third little chicken,
With a sharp little squeal,
'I wish that I could find myself,
Some nice yellow meal.'

Said the fourth little chicken,
With a small sigh of grief,
'I wish that I could find myself,
A delicious green leaf.'

Said the fifth little chicken,
With a screechy little cry,
'I wish that I could find myself,
A dainty little fly.'

Said the sixth little chicken,
With a faint little moan,
'I wish that I could find myself,
A wee gravel stone.'

'Now, see here!' said the mother hen,
From the green garden patch,
'If you want your breakfast, little chicks,
Come over here and scratch!'

In an effort to make poetry important and enjoyable for young children the teacher might select a particular poem and:

- read it in different ways, using different voices and intonations, varying the pace and rhythm;
- record the reading (by the teacher or by the whole class) and leave a taped version for further listening;
- ask the children to talk about the theme and relate to their own experiences;
- mount a copy next to pictures and photographs of the theme;
- explore how sounds of words reflect their meaning;
- encourage the children to mime actions described;
- encourage the children to think up news rhymes and word pairings;
- ask questions about it – *factual* ('How many different kinds of food do the six little chicks like to eat?'), *speculative* ('What or who comes looking for the hairy toe?') or to *elicit a personal response* ('Which of Auntie Penny's pets do you like the most?');
- discuss word patterns, unusual spellings, interesting rhymes;
- provide copies so that the children can work on their own readings in pairs or groups;
- use drama activities: improvisation, tableaux and hot seating to explore the theme;
- encourage children to illustrate it or part of it and use this as a basis for further discussion of the verse;
- cover parts of it and ask the children to suggest appropriate words and phrases.

Chapter 8
Responding to Poetry at Key Stage 2

All poetry is magic. It is a spell against insensitivity, failure of imagination, ignorance and barbarism. The way that a good poem 'works' on a reader is as mysterious, as hard to explain, as the possible working of a charm or spell. A poem is much more than a mere arrangements of words on paper, or on the tongue. Its hints, suggestions, the echoes it sets off in the mind, and its omissions (what a poet decides to leave out is often just as important as what he puts in) all join up with the reader's thoughts and feelings and make a kind of magical union.

(Causley 1990)

From their first week in school children should be exposed to a wide range of poems. Pupils are expected, at all ages, to read poetry aloud and silently, to talk about their preferences for particular poems and be given the opportunity to write their own poetry and experiment with different forms, rhythms, rhymes and verse structures.

Poetry needs to be at the heart of the work in English because of the quality of the language at work on experience that it offers us. If language becomes separated from the moral and emotional life – becomes merely a trail of clichés which neither communicate with nor quicken the mind of the reader – then we run the risk of depriving children of the kind of vital resource of language which poetry provides.

(DES 1987)

The selection of poems which follow includes a range of verse forms written by children at Key Stage 2. They were helped in the shaping of their own experiences by looking carefully at the poems of other writers and by using these poems as models for their own writing. They were encouraged to imitate the style and structure of a particular writer. This modelling technique acts as a 'scaffold' on which children are able to build, using their own ideas and language.

Miniature poems

Poets, like artists, look carefully at their subjects, then select the best words to describe them. They put down on paper the pictures or images which come into their minds and try to make their listeners or readers feel as closely as possible to the way they feel about a person or animal or scene. Sometimes the poems are long and detailed but at other times they are short and vivid. Year 4 children studied the following four superbly illustrated short poems produced by The Poetry Society on a large colourful poster:

- *Cow* by Karla Kuskin in *Near the Window Tree*, Harper and Row;
- *Pig* by Paul Eluard in *Lizard Over Ice*, edited by Gervase Phinn, Thomas Nelson;
- *Tiger* by Judith Nicholls in *Midnight Forest*, Faber and Faber;
- *Ants* by Tatsuji Miyoshi in *An Anthology of Modern Japanese Poetry*, edited by I. Kono and R. Fukada, Kenkyusha Ltd.

In these 'miniature' poems, the poets try to capture exactly in a few lines an image of a cow, pig, tiger and an army of industrious ants. Metaphor, simile and imagery work powerfully in a few words to release rich associations in the mind of the readers and recreate the creatures with a fresh perspective. Commonplace words are shifted from a familiar context to a new and original one to create a vivid and unusual effect.

The approach to studying the poems was as follows:

- Before reading the poems the teacher gathered the children around her and wrote the names of the four animals on the board. She asked the children to attempt a short description of each – intended for someone who has never seen such creatures before. The poster was then displayed and the four poems were read in silence by the children and then a second time by the teacher. Finally the poems were read aloud together by the teacher and children. It is important that poems are fully appreciated before they are analysed and reading them three times gives them a chance to 'breathe' and for the children to get a feel for the rhymes and rhythms.
- There followed a discussion on how each poet managed to capture the 'essence' of the creature in a few, carefully-selected words. This developed into a consideration of how the poets used similes and metaphors to create a picture of the creatures. In *Pig* Paul Eluard compares the animal's head to a cannon and in *The Ground*, Tatsuji Miyoshi compares the butterfly's wings to the sails of a yacht. In her poem, Karla Kuskin uses a striking and unusual metaphor of the cow – 'a big fur box on legs.'
- The children were asked to compare the lives of these creatures. In *Cow* and *Pig* there is a feeling of contentedness and stability, but in *Tiger* there is a sense of sadness as the caged creature longs for its freedom. The teacher focused on *Tiger* and asked the children to describe their own experiences and feelings when visiting a zoo. Teacher and children then wrote together a short vivid description of the cage and what the tiger was doing, trying to get inside the mind of the animal and recreate the thoughts of its present condition and memories of its past life in the jungle.

- The children were encouraged to create their own very short poem on an animal. They jotted down any words or phrases and decided on one clear image which created a picture in miniature. The children were encouraged to use metaphors and similes to create interesting pictures in their own poems. They were asked to produce a first draft, stressing that the poem should not rhyme and should only be three or four lines in length. Here are some examples written by pupils aged eight and nine:

Dog
Lazy bag of bones,
Hairy sack on the sofa,
Plump as a fat old cushion,
Round as a barrel.

Gerbil
Furry face,
Bright eyes,
Cheeky chops,
Naughty nibbler.

Slug
Slimy slitherer,
Shiny sneaker,
Oozing across the wall
Like a runny nose.

Polar Bear
White as the snow,
Cold as the wind,
Big as the iceberg,
Strong as the sea.

- The children illustrated their poems using paint, pencils and ink, collage materials or charcoal. A display of the illustrations alongside the poems provided starting points for further discussion.
- The four animal poems and the children's efforts were compared with others on the same theme. There are lots of animal poems in the following collections: *Evidence of Elephants* by Gerard Benson, Viking Kestrel; *Condensed Animals* by Spike Milligan, Puffin; *Say Hello to the Buffalo and Other Animals* by Miles Gibson, Heinemann, and *Animal Verse* compiled by Raymond Wilson, Beaver Books.
- Year 6 children were asked to write some 'miniature' poems on a range of themes. In the following collections are many examples of very short poems which offer excellent models:
  Splinters, compiled by Michael Harrison, Oxford University Press;
  The Song That Sings the Bird, compiled by Ruth Craft, Collins;
  Big World, Little World, compiled by Sue Stewart, Nelson;
  All the Small Poems by Valerie Worth, Farrar, Straus and Giroux;
  River Winding by Charlotte Zolotow, Blackie and Son;
  A Cup of Starshine, edited by Jill Bennett, Puffin.

Below are some 'miniature' poems composed by Year 5 and 6 children:

Icicles
Dangling daggers,
Slippery spikes,
Icy horns.
Winter's fangs.

Forest
Tall firs,
Sharp spears,
Like pointed pencils
They puncture the sky.

Traffic
Huffing, puffing,
Coughing, growling,
Chuddering, juddering,
Cars in a queue, lorries in a line.

Scissors
Shiny slicers
Silver snippers,
Snip-snap, snip-snap,
Like the legs of a dangerous dancer.

Sea Shells
Smooth and white like icing sugar,
Hard and yellow like old toenails,
Shiny and pink like sweets,
Round and black like eyeballs.

Castle
Cold grey stone.
Stands alone,
With towering keep,
And dungeons deep.

Patterned poems

In the collections recommended earlier in this book are many patterned poems ideal for discussion and study and which offer excellent models or 'scaffolds' for the children's own writing. Children might be encouraged to try a miniature word picture which follows one of the following fixed patterns.

The *haiku* is a seasonal Japanese poem of three lines, usually written as seventeen syllables. The first line (five syllables) sets the scene, the second line (seven syllables) introduces some action and the third line (5 syllables) 'fuses' the two – bring the scene setting and the action together. The simplicity of the haiku is the result of great discipline and the things left unsaid can be more important than what is on the page.

Below are four haiku written by Year 5 and 6 children:

Spring
Still water. White yachts
Stand like picnic sandwiches
On the quiet lake.

Summer
Hot day. Burning sun
Dries the soil to yellow dust
And toasts the pavements.

Autumn
Strong wind. Whips up leaves,
Blows the washing off the line,
And roars with pleasure.

Winter
Rough sea. Seagulls twirl
Like paper in the wind
Above the water.

The *senryu* is named after the eighteenth century Japanese poet, Karai Senryu, and is a three line verse similar to the haiku. Like the haiku it often has a seasonal reference, but it is different in that the senryu disregards rigid rules and is more humorous in content.

The following amusing short, sharp senryu were written by Year 6 children:

When the sun shines
And the birds sing in the summer trees –
I stay in bed.

Icy roads, thick snow,
No school!
Hey ho!

Another Japanese form of verse is the *tanka*, composed of five lines of thirty one syllables. As with the haiku, traditionally the theme centres on lyrical subjects of nature, love and loss and there is often a quick turn at the end of the poem. It follows a particular pattern;

Line 1 : five syllables
Line 2 : seven syllables
Line 3 : five syllables
Line 4 : seven syllables
Line 5 : seven syllables

Here are three tanka composed by Year 6 children:

Old house in Winter,
Dark and cold and full of dust,
Rotten window frames,
Leaking roof and rising damp,
The home of spooks and spectres.

Spring in the forest.
Buds bursting from the dark trees.
Bushes thick and green.
A carpet of bluebells bright,
And hawthorns blossom.

Sweltering Summer!
Bright red arms and sore, sore legs.
Cooking in the sun.
Sand so hot it burns your toes,
Sea so cold your feet sizzle.

Another miniature and carefully patterned poem is five lines of the *cinquain*, which describes a single experience. It has the following pattern:

Line 1 : The topic (two syllables)
Line 2 : Describes the topic (four syllables)
Line 3 : Expresses some action (six syllables)
Line 4 : Expresses a feeling or makes a statement (eight syllables)
Line 5 : Sums up the topic (two syllables)

Here are two of my own cinquains which were used as models for the children:

Old house,
So dark, so cold.
A musty smell of mould
And giant shivering shadows
Waiting.

A light
Under the door.
A whispering inside.
I run back up the stairs in fright –
Phantoms!

The following cinquains were written by Year 6 children:

School –
Crowded corridors,
Silent, endless lessons,
Long hours of listening,
Boredom.

Station –
Smoky black,
Round, ribbed roof,
smell of oily trains,
Mystery.

Dentist –
Bright eyed.
Peering, probing, prodding.
Testing his drill.
Terror!

Fox –
Red robber.
Sneaking, stalking, stealing.
Hiding from the Hunt,
Cunning.

A more demanding and difficult poem to write is the *diamont*, a seven line verse written in the shape of a diamond and which contains a contrast of ideas or descriptions. It has the following pattern:

Line 1 : The topic (one word)
Line 2 : Describes the topic (two words)
Line 3 : Expresses some action (three words)
Line 4 : Relates to the topic (four words)
Line 5 : Relates to the opposite of the topic (three words)
Line 6 : Describes the opposite of the topic (two words)
Line 7 : Is the opposite of the topic (three word)

Before attempting their own diamont poems children might be given a series of contrasting ideas or opposites to think about:

young and old   fast and slow
big and small   rich and poor
dark and light   hot and cold
Summer and Winter   wet and dry

The following poems were written by Year 6 pupils:

Morning.
Bright light.
Waking, stretching, yawning.
Clear, fresh, sunny, warm.
Dark, cold, silent.
Pitch black.
Evening.

Baby.
Bright eyes.
Dribbling, gurgling, whimpering,
Sleeping, yawning, waking, crying.
Sleeping, yawning, waking.
Dull eyes.
Grandpa.

Kennings

The word *kenning* comes from the Old Norse and is a verse form where one thing is described in terms of another. Kennings provide excellent opportunities for pupils to use their imaginations to the full and develop their observational skills. An excellent example of this verse form is John Agard's *Don't Call Alligator Long Mouth Till You Cross the River* which appears in his collection, *Say it Again, Granny*, Bodley Head. Ask the children to write their own kennings. They should decided on a subject, discuss the idea with a partner, jot down ideas as soon as they come into their heads and attempt to create a short word picture or image. They might use repetitions and rhymes, metaphors and similes to make the poem vivid and unusual and devise a clever and amusing ending.

Below are four kennings written by Year 5 and 6 children.

Shark	**Hedgehog**
Razor teeth	Prickle ball,
Grey missile	Bristle back
Button eye	Brush face
Sharp fin	Sharp spines
Cold killer	Night snuffler
Sea scavenger	Flea bag.
Dustbin of the deep.	

Vulture	**Dad**
I am the patient watcher	Loud laugher
Old Dusty feathers	Scary shouter
Bald head	Dangerous dancer
Big beak	Dreadful dresser
Bare neck	Car crasher
Sharp eye	Silly smiler
Bone picker	Noisy snorer
Body snatcher	Fast eater
Bird of Death.	Old softie.

Calligrams

The way poems are arranged is important. In *Allivator*, which appears in the anthology *An Imaginary Menagerie*, Roger McGough's words appear long and narrow and move in steps from bottom to the top just like an elevator. In *Waves* by Jackie Kay in *The Puffin Book of Utterly Brilliant Poetry*, edited by Brian Patten, the words move up and down across the page like a sea swell. *Calligrams*, sometimes called *shape poems* or *concrete verse*, can stimulate children to use their imaginations and appreciate how arrangement of the words on the page creates the impression of the chosen subject. Prior to writing their own calligrams, a group of Year 5 and 6 pupils looked at a selection which included:

Frogspawn by Peter Dixon in *Grow Your Own Poems*, Macmillan;

The Honey Pot by Alan Ridell in *Eclipse*, John Calder Publications;

The Kite by June Crebbin in *The Jungle Sale*, Viking Kestrel;

Downpour by Christine Bentley in *Lizard Over Ice*, edited by Gervase Phinn, Thomas Nelson;

Holiday Memories by Paula Davies in *Word Whirls and Other Shape Poems*, edited by John Foster, Oxford University Press;

What's in a Shape? in *Picture a Poem* by Gina Douthwaite, Red Fox.

A group of children produced some shape poems based on parts of the body (eyes, feet, hands, nose), fruit (pineapple, banana, pear, apple), animals (cat, elephant, giraffe, hedgehog), fish (shark, starfish, eel, jellyfish) and various shapes (star, diamond, crown, heart). Alice and Mark produced four shape poems using the computer and based them on well-known proverbs provided by the teacher: *All's well that ends well, He who laughs last, laughs longest, Birds of a feather flock together* and *Every cloud has a silver lining.*

```
                                              lining
        Well                                  CLOUD
        well                       lining            lining
        well                       CLOUD             CLOUD
        well                       lining               lining
        well                       CLOUD                CLOUD
        well                  lining                       lining
        well                  CLOUD                           CLOUD
        well                       lining                lining
        well                       CLOUD                CLOUD
        well                            lining
        Well                            CLOUD
```

```
Laugh ..... Laugh ..... Laugh ..... Laugh ..... Laugh ..... Laugh
Laugh ..... Laugh ..... Laugh ..... Laugh ..... Laugh ..... L  a  u  g  h
```

```
   BIRDSBIRDSBIRDSBIRDSBIRDSBIRDSBIRDSBIRDSBIRDS
        BIRDSBIRDSBIRDSBIRDSBIRDSBIRDS
            BIRDSBIRDSBIRDSBIRDS
              BIRDSBIRDSBIRDS
                BIRDSBIRDS
                  BIRDS
```

Wordplay

In *Allivator* Roger McGough invents his poem creature (a cross between an alligator and an elevator) by a clever combination of words which links two apparently very different things together. Children could attempt something similar on the lines of the following written by John, aged eleven, who was inspired to write a whole booklet of imaginary animals.

I'm smooth and brown and nice to eat,
With crunchy jaws and munchy feet,
I'm guaranteed to make you smile,
I am the hungry **chocodile**.

I'm greasy and I'm rather chubby,
Good to eat and very tubby,
Sprinkle salt upon my tummy,
And you'll find me yummy, yummy,
But you'll not get me in a bus –
I am the **chipopotomus**.

Everyone avoids me.
The reason is plain to see.
I wobble, wobble, pant and pant.
I am the frightening **jellyphant**.

Clerihews

A *clerihew* is a comic, rhyming, four-line verse, typically about a person named in one of the lines. Here are three traditional verses and two of my own which show different rhyming patterns:

Elsie Marley is grown so fine,	(a)
She won't get up to feed the swine.	(a)
She lies in bed till eight or nine,	(a)
Lazy Elsie Marley.	(b)

The elephant carries a great big trunk;	(a)
He never packs it with his clothes	(b)
It has no lock and it has no key,	(c)
But he takes it with him wherever he goes.	(b)

I often sit and wish that I	(a)
Could be a kite up in the sky,	(a)
And ride upon the breeze and go,	(b)
Whichever way I chanced to blow.	(b)

Elizabeth said, 'I'm like a queen,	(a)
In my new dress of vivid green',	(a)
Her brother Matt let out a scream,	(a)
'You're a wee bit early for Halloween!'	(a)

'Do you want a smacked bottom my lad?'	(a)
Asked my father in threatening voice.	(b)
I'm not likely to say: 'Yes please, Dad,'	(a)
I don't think I've much of a choice!	(b)

Poets use rhyme to gain our attention, give pattern to the verse and create a pleasing musical effect. Children love short comic rhymes and clerihews are ideal for teaching about rhyme schemes and patterns. Give the children a selection of clerihews and ask them to work out the different rhyme schemes. Encourage children to write their own clerihews. They can use a rhyming dictionary to help them.

Acrostic poems

Acrostics are puzzle poems in which the beginning, middle or last letters of each line form the word vertically. Children enjoy writing acrostics. They offer a clear pattern and are fun to devise. Look at a selection of acrostics with the children and discuss the poets' choice of words and how they manage to capture the very essence of the person, place or creature. John Cunliffe's collection *Standing on a Strawberry*, published by Andre Deutsch, has some fine examples of acrostic poems as does Judith Nicholl's anthology *Midnight Forest*, published by Faber and Faber. *Monday* from *Junk Mail* by Michael Harrison, Oxford University Press and *Love Letter* in *Love Shouts and Whispers* by Vernon Scannell, Hutchinson, will elicit a lively response. Encourage the children to write their own acrostics trying to capture the essential features of their chosen subject. They might pick:

   a name – their own, a friend, brother, sister, uncle or aunt;
   an animal – lion, mouse, shrew, prehistoric creature;
   an insect – ant, caterpillar, butterfly, wasp, bee;
   a mood or feeling – rage, terror, loneliness, love;
   a place – village, market, town, country;
   a building – school, castle, factory, hospital.

Having read a small selection of acrostics, we then tried our hand at writing our own. Claire wrote *Dog and Cat*, Russell and William produced the clever and imaginative *Skyscraper* and Julia and Terri the two verses, *Nessie* and *Dragon*. *Yeti* and *Banshee* are my own.

Dog and Cat
Dangerous
Old
Grumbler.

Claws
And
Teeth.

Skyscraper
Soaring high,
King of the sky.
You are the tallest,
Swaying in space.
Cloud topped tower,
Rising from the ground,
Above everything,
Perhaps one day
Reaching the skies.

Nessie

Night came.
Everyone was in bed
Sleeping,
Snoring.
In the loch
Enormous creatures swam.

Yeti

You
Enormous
Tibetan
Iceman

Dragon

Down in the forest,
Roaring in his den,
A fire breathing creature,
Gobbles up the men.
Only princes strong and brave
Never get eaten in his cave.

Banshee

Bar the door
And bolt the shutter.
No-one stir,
Speak or mutter.
Hark! Can you hear it,
Eerily howling,
Endlessly prowling?

Riddles

Words can be tricky and troublesome things at times – particularly when poets use them to write *riddles*. Riddles are word puzzles, very cleverly written and fun to work out. Some riddles are of one line, other are long and detailed; some are easy to solve and others very difficult; some are 900 years old, others very modern; some rhyme, others don't; and they come from many parts of the world, written in many different languages. The following collections have some unusual and cleverly written riddles guaranteed to intrigue:

Talking to the Sun, selected by Kenneth Koch and Kate Farrell, Viking Kestrel;
Catching a Spider by John Mole, Blackie;
Word Spells by Judith Nicholls, Faber and Faber;
Third Time Lucky by Mick Gowar, Viking Kestrel;
Pudmuddle Jump In edited by Beverley Mathias, Methuen.

The following traditional poem is ideal for explaining to children exactly how a riddle works:

Have you ever seen a sheet on a river bed?
Or a single hair from a hammer's head?
Has the foot of a mountain any toes?
And is there a pair of garden hose?

Does the needle ever wink its eye?
Why doesn't the wing of a building fly?
Can you tickle the ribs of a parasol?
Or open the trunk of a tree at all?

Are the teeth of a rake ever going to bite?
Have the hands of clock any left or right?
Can the garden plot be deep and dark?
And what is the sound of the oak tree's bark?

Look at a selection of riddles with the children and discuss the poets' clever use of words, particularly their use of puns. An excellent text for infants is: *Riddling Rhymes for Small Children* by Delphine Evans, Beaver Books and for juniors any collection by the master 'riddler' John Mole will appeal and fascinate.

- Give the children (in pairs or groups) a series of riddles with no solutions. Ask them to try and solve the word puzzles.
- Ask the children (again in pairs or small groups) to list words that have double meanings and could be used in a riddle, words like *jacket, eye, face, hand, finger, foot, leaf, boot, bed, arm, leg, head, neck, seat*. With the full class write a few riddles.
- Children might be asked to write some riddles of their own, the more ingenious the better. They need to decide on a subject:

Object: knife, hammer, telephone, scissors
Animal: horse, pig, crocodile, elephant
Element :   water, fire, wind
Plant: onion, cabbage, carrot, dandelion clock
Transport: train, bus, bicycle, aeroplane

Having discussed the main features of the subject and jotted down ideas they then try to create a word picture or image, using metaphors and similes to make the riddle vivid, unusual and challenging. Children could attempt something similar on the lines of the following, written by Year 6 children.

Riddle 1

I'm a real square!
Dry as dust,
Grey as stone
Paper thin and perforated
In hot water my flavour burst
I am the quencher of thirsts
What am I?
(teabag)

Riddle 2

Metal slider
Noisy snake
Smelly transporter
Comfortable carrier
Singing on the rails
(train)

Riddle 3

I have a face, but not a mouth
I have hands but no arms
I can stand but cannot sit
And I go on for hours and hours
(grandfather clock)

Riddle 4

I'm an icy blossom
A tiny piece of frozen paper
A cold white petal,
A winter pattern.
(snowflake)

Ballads

Poets not only describe what they see and hear around them, their feelings and thoughts, wishes and sensations, they also use poetry to tell stories or narratives. One form of narrative verse has its roots in story telling and song and this is the *ballad*. The earliest narrative poems in English were ballads, anonymously written and passed down from generation to generation by word of mouth. *Lord Ullin's Daughter* by Thomas Campbell, is typical of a ballad poem. It has a regular rhyme scheme of ABAB and a regular rhythm of 4:3:4:3 beats to a verse of four lines. Like the ballads written 400 years ago, this poem has the same pounding rhythm, fast action, stark simplicity of detail and characterisation, frequent repetition of words, snatches of dramatic dialogue and the familiar tragic end. These qualities make the ballad excellent for reading aloud.

Lord Ullin's Daughter

A chieftain to the Highlands bound,
Cries, 'Boatman, do not tarry!
And I'll give thee a silver pound
To row us o'er the ferry.'

Now who be ye, would cross Lochgyle,
This dark and stormy water?'
'Oh, I am the chief of Ulva's isle,
And this Lord Ullin's daughter...'

And fast before her father's men
Three days we've fled together;
For should he find us in the glen,
My blood would stain the heather.

His horsemen hard behind us ride:
Should they our step discover,
Then who will cheer my bonny bride
When they have slain her lover?'

Out spoke the hardy highland wight,
'I'll go my chief – I'm ready.
It is not for your silver bright,
But for your winsome lady.

And by my word, the bonny bird
In danger shall not tarry;
So though the waves are raging white,
I'll row you o'er the ferry.'

By this the storm grew loud apace;
The water-wraith was shrieking;
And in the scowl of heaven each face
Grew dark as they were speaking.

But still as wilder blew the wind,
And as the night grew dearer,
Adown the glen rode armoured men –
Their trampling sounded nearer.

'O haste thee, haste!' the lady cries,
'Though tempests round us gather;
I'll meet the raging of the skies,
But not an angry father.'

The boat has left a stormy land,
A stormy sea before her –
When, O! too strong for human hand,
The tempest gathered o'er her.

And still they rowed amidst the roar
Of waters fast prevailing –
Lord Ullin reached the fatal shore;
His wrath was changed to wailing.

For sore dismayed through storm and shade
His child he did discover;
One lovely hand she stretched for aid,
And one was round her lover.

'Come back! Come back!' he cried in grief,
Across the stormy water.
'And I'll forgive your Highland chief,
My daughter ' – O my daughter!'

'Twas vain – the loud waves lashed the shore,
Return or aid preventing.
The waters wild went o'er his child,
And he was left lamenting.

- Read a selection of ballads with the children. Ones which make compelling listening are *The Ballad of Johnny Shiner* by John Cunliffe in the anthology *Standing on a Strawberry*, Andre Deutsch; *The Highwayman* by Alfred Noyes, *The Pied Piper of Hamelin* by Robert Browning and *The Forsaken Merman* by Matthew Arnold in *The Oxford Book of Story Poems*, Oxford University Press.
- Discuss the structure and characteristics of this form of verse: the subject, rhyme scheme, rhythm, number of verses, verse length, choice of words, use of dialogue.
- Ask the children to try writing a ballad. They might relate the story of something they have heard on the television or read about in a newspaper or they might recount an incident which happened at school.
- Ask the children to write out a ballad in the form of a story or play.
- *Lord Ullin's Daughter* could be acted out or performed as a reading.
- Read *The Legend of the Lambton Worm*, a poem I wrote and which is based on the famous Northern legend. Compare it with the prose version, illustrated by the

Sunderland artist Joan Henderson and published by the Newcastle-upon-Tyne City Libraries and Arts (ISBN 0 90265368 7).

- Read the poem version of *The Legend of the Lambton Worm* and encourage the children to prepare and present it. Ask them to share their opinions and challenge them to justify their points of view by reference to the text. Use specialist terminology to provide the language for talking about the poem: *theme, mood, rhythm, syllable, rhyme, metre, imagery, verse, figures of speech* and encourage the children to discuss the language: the choice of particular words and phrases (for example powerful, expressive verbs and vivid adjectives), lack of detail, repetition, the simple verse structure and the use of punctuation.

The Legend of the Lambton Worm
There's a very famous story
About a serpent and a well:
The story of The Lambton Worm,
A story I will tell.

It happened one fine Monday,
In a forest near a lake,
That the Lord of Lambton Castle,
Came upon a snake.

It was a tiny, wriggly thing,
With a rather fishy smell,
So the Lord of Lambton Castle,
Dropped it down a nearby well.

Then he forgot about it,
And went fighting far away,
But the worm it grew and grew and grew
To be slimy, fat and grey.

One day it slithered from the well,
And roaring like a leopard,
It swallowed up a flock of sheep,
The sheepdog and the shepherd.

For years and years the creature lived
Devouring all it saw,
When one day, brave Lord Lambton
Came back from the war.

He put his helmet on his head
And with his sword and shield,
He climbed up every mountain
And looked in every field.

Until he found the Lambton Worm
With eyes a fiery red,
And he lifted up his great sharp sword
And chopped off the big black head.

Then he cut it into pieces
And he dropped it down the well,
And that was the end of the Lambton Worm,
So storytellers tell!

Conversation poems

Children enjoy reading poems in twos and threes, lifting the verses from the page and performing them for others. There is a wide range of conversation poems about pupils and teachers, brothers and sisters, mums and dads, grannies and grandpas, animals and ghosts, in a range of styles and moods and of varying length. Year 5 and 6 children were asked to select a poem from the following and prepare it for performance in front of the class:

Storytime by Judith Nicholls in *Midnight Forest*, Faber and Faber;
O, What is that Sound? by W.H. Auden in *Collected Poems*, Faber and Faber;
You Can't Be That by Brian Patten in *Thawing Frozen Frogs*, Viking Books;
Schooltalk by Christine Bentley in *Five Themes for English*, edited by Gervase Phinn, Longman;
Look – said the Boy by Michael Rosen in *Wouldn't You Like to Know*, Scholastic Publications;
Silverfish Rap by Rowena Sommerville in *Don't Step on That Earwig*, compiled and illustrated by the author, Red Fox;
My Dad. Your Dad by Kit Wright from *Rabbiting On*, Harper-Collins;
A Christmas Story by Gervase Phinn in Classroom Creatures, Roselea Publications.

The children worked in pairs, then tried their hands at writing their own conversation poems. I gave them a set of guidelines to help them:
Your conversation poem:

- Might be in the form of a letter – to an auntie, the Electricity Board, a neighbour, pen-friend, the head teacher, a supermarket manager;
- Could be a telephone poem to a doctor, dentist, teacher, relation, neighbour or friend;
- Might be a conversation between:
    Mum or dad and a neighbour,
    Two angry motorists,
    A policeman and a burglar,
    A king or queen and a beggar,
    A pupil and a teacher,
    Two pupils,
    A mum or dad and a daughter or son,
    Two animals,
    Two ghosts,
    The wind and the sea . . .
- Needs to be rehearsed for performance – try out different voices.

Here are two conversation poems, the first written by John, aged eleven, and the second by myself:

Interview with the Head Teacher

Teacher:	I want to see you, Whiting!
Pupil:	Yes, sir?
Teacher:	What about this window, Whiting?
Pupil:	What window would that be, sir?
Teacher:	This window here, Whiting.
Pupil:	Oh, that window, sir.
Teacher:	What happened, Whiting?
Pupil:	Happened, sir?
Teacher:	To the window, Whiting!
Pupil:	It's broken, sir.
Teacher:	I know it's broken, Whiting!
Pupil:	Yes sir.
Teacher:	Why is it broken, Whiting?
Pupil:	I think a bird flew into it, sir.
Teacher:	A bird, Whiting.
Pupil:	Flew into it, sir.
Teacher:	What?
Pupil:	A bird, sir.
Teacher:	A bird, Whiting?
Pupil:	Flew into it, sir.
Teacher:	What sort of bird, Whiting?
Pupil:	I believe it was an eagle, sir.
Teacher:	An eagle, Whiting.
Pupil:	A golden eagle, sir.
Teacher:	And what was a golden eagle doing around school, Whiting?
Pupil:	Flying I think, sir?
Teacher:	Why was a golden eagle flying around school, Whiting?
Pupil:	Because it couldn't be bothered to walk, sir?
Teacher:	Are you being cheeky, Whiting?
Pupil:	No sir.
Teacher:	I think you are, Whiting.
Pupil:	Watch out, sir.
Teacher:	What is it, Whiting?
Pupil:	An eagle, sir.
Teacher:	An eagle, Whiting?
Pupil:	Swooping down towards you, sir.
Teacher:	Where, Whiting?
Pupil:	There, sir.
Teacher (as he is carried off):	AAAAAaaaaaaaahhhhhhhhh!
Pupil:	I did tell you ...sir.

Interrogation in the Nursery

Infant:	What's that?
School Inspector:	What?
Infant:	That on your face?
School Inspector:	It's a moustache.
Infant:	What does it do?
School Inspector:	It doesn't do anything.
Infant:	Oh.
School Inspector:	It just sits there on my lip.
Infant:	Does it go up your nose?
School Inspector:	No.
Infant:	Could I stroke it?
School Inspector:	No.
Infant:	Is it alive?
School Inspector:	No, it's not alive.
Infant:	Can I have one?
School Inspector:	No, little girls don't have moustaches.
Infant:	Why?
School Inspector:	Well, they just don't.
Infant:	Can I have one when I grow up?
School Inspector:	No, ladies don't have moustaches either.
Infant:	Well, my grannie's got one!

Poems with rhythm

All poems have a rhythm, a pattern of beats or sounds. Some poems have a slow, stately rhythm, others a regular, sing-song rhythm. Start by reading a selection of rhythmic poems which might include:

Seaside Song by John Rice in *Lizard Over Ice*, edited by Gervase Phinn, Thomas Nelson;

The Want-Want Twins by Jackie Kay in *Three Has Gone*, Blackie;

Red Boot On by Kit Wright in *Lizard Over Ice*, edited by Gervase Phinn, Thomas Nelson;

Talking Turkeys!! by Benjamin Zephaniah, in *Talking Turkeys*, Viking;

Daniel by Vachel Lindsay in *Lizard Over Ice*, edited by Gervase Phinn, Thomas Nelson;

Tell Me, Tell Me, Sarah Jane by Charles Causley in *Figgie Hobbin*, Macmillan.

Ask the children to prepare one of the poems for performance.

A poem might be studied at greater depth, for example, *The Owl and Pussy-cat* by Edward Lear. This is a richly original and entertaining piece of comic verse, with a strong verbal pattern, catchy rhymes and a boisterous, engaging rhythm. Children down the years have loved the affectionate humour, cleverness of the language, the rhymes and rhythms and the wonderfully exaggerated characters.

The Owl and the Pussy-cat

The Owl and the Pussy-cat went to sea
In a beautiful pea-green boat,
They took some honey, and plenty of money,
Wrapped up in a five-pound note.
The Owl looked up to the stars above,
And sang to a small guitar,
'O lovely Pussy! O Pussy, my love,
What a beautiful Pussy you are,
You are,
You are!
What a beautiful Pussy you are!'

Pussy said the Owl, 'You elegant fowl!
How charmingly sweet you sing!
O let us me married! too long we have tarried:
But what shall we do for a ring?'
They sailed away for a year and a day,
To the land where the Bong-tree grows,
And there in a wood a Piggy-wig stood,
With a ring at the end of his nose,
His nose,
His nose,
With a ring at the end of his nose.

'Dear Pig, are you willing to sell for a shilling
Your ring?' Said the Piggy, 'I will.'
So they took it away, and were married next day
By the Turkey who lived on the hill.
They dined on mince, and slices of quince,
Which they ate with a runcible spoon;
And hand in hand, on the edge of the sand,
They danced by the light of the moon,
The moon,
The moon,
They danced by the light of the moon.

- In reading the poem the musical vitality of the verse needs to be brought out. This poem can be read in a loud confident voice – perhaps as a choral performance by the class – to bring out the rhythm. Children, working in pairs or small groups, might consider the pace, expression, number of voices, background sounds and movement of the poem. In small groups encourage the children to practise different ways of performing the poem: quickly, slowly, loudly, softly, stressing different words, clapping their hands or clicking their fingers to establish the beat, reading in pairs or as a chorus or maybe using mime.
- Highlight the poem's imagery, unusual or invented words and repetitions. Ask the children to describe the 'bong tree' and the 'runcible spoon'. Look at the other brilliantly conceived and highly original poem *Jabberwocky* by Lewis Carroll where there is a whole host of invented words and creatures.

- Ask the children to list a series of questions that they might ask Edward Lear about his poem if he were alive. A surprising number of unusual and unexpected questions will emerge.

Poems with rhyme

Poets use rhyme to get our attention or to make us listen or to create a pleasing musical effect. Rhyme can also give pattern to the verses of a poem. Start by reading a selection of rhyming poems which might include:

School Trip in *Classroom Creatures* by Gervase Phinn, Roselea Publications;
The Cat and the Pig by Gerard Benson in *The Magnificent Callisto*, Blackie;
Dinner Time Rhyme by June Crebbin in *The Jungle Sale*, Viking;
Moby Duck by Terry Jones in *Funny Bunch*, edited by Kit Wright, Puffin.

I have often used one of my own poems to initiate a discussion about rhyming verse, sometimes omitting certain words and asking the children to complete the poem with appropriate rhymes.

As You Were
Soft as fur, hard as iron,
Timid as a mouse, brave as a lion.
Weak as water, strong as an ox,
Round as a ring, square as a box.
Lazy as a lizard, busy as a bee,
High as the mountains, deep as the sea.
Dead as a doornail, live as a wire,
Cold as an iceberg, hot as fire.
Bright as sunshine, dull as a stone,
Wet as a raindrop, dry as a bone.
Heavy as lead, light as a feather,
Smooth as silk, tough as old leather.
Small as an ant, big as a whale,
Fast as a ferret, slow as a snail.
Thin as a beanpole, thick as a rope,
Safe as houses, slippery as soap.
Dark as a mine shaft, clear as light,
Loud as thunder, quiet as the night.
Happy as dad and happy as mum,
Happy as me when the holidays come!

A poem might be studied at greater depth, for example *The Eagle* by Alfred Lord Tennyson. Tennyson was one of the giants of Victorian English poetry and his skill and versatility as a craftsman of verse have rarely been equalled. *The Eagle* is perhaps the most well-known and popular of his short lyrics. The musical quality is created largely through the use of rhyme and rhythm which bring the words sharply to our attention.

The Eagle
He clasps the crag with crooked hands;
Close to the sun in lonely lands,
Ringed with the azure world he stands.

The wrinkled sea beneath him crawls;
He watches from his mountain walls,
And like a thunderbolt he falls.

- With the first exploration of this poem the children should be encouraged to read it quietly to themselves before hearing a reading by the teacher. There should be no attempt on the part of the teacher to explain a phrase or image which seems perplexing or obscure. Encourage a response by talking about whether it is a fast or a slow moving poem or a mixture of both. Let the children see the pattern of words on the page before you read it. Try reading the poem slowly to give the verse time to expand and exert its musical quality, asking the children to listen carefully to the rhymes. Such activities develop active listening skills and encourage a thoughtful response.
- Sequencing requires a close examination of a poem's structure. For example, the six lines of this poem might be cut up and given to the children to arrange in an alternative order. It is interesting that the effect of the verse changes dramatically when the lines are re-ordered.
- To encourage the children to think about the choice of words and the imagery in the poem, present them with a copy with significant words omitted. Then ask them, working in pairs, to find an appropriate word of the right number of syllables to complete the poem. Stress that the poet's choice of words is not necessarily the right or the best one. This activity, which can be used with any poem or piece of prose, encourages children to engage actively with the text and consider the writing in an interesting and creative way.
- Rhyme consists of two words or syllables of words which sound alike, except for the initial consonant sound. In *The Eagle* the rhyme scheme of AAABBB is simple but effective. This poem is an ideal vehicle for explaining to children what is meant by a rhyme scheme and for introducing them to some poetic vocabulary and figurative language: rhyming couplets, quatrains, full rhymes, half-rhymes, alliteration, simile, personification, assonance and metre.
- Encourage the children to experiment with alliteration. Tennyson links one word with another and one idea with another by the deliberate repetition of a consonant sound. This alliteration is used not for its own sake but in order to imitate the sound of the thing being described. There are many hard sounds associated with the eagle: 'clasps', 'crag', 'crooked' and 'crawls' – which contrast with the soft sounds associated with the expanse of sea and sky: 'lonely', 'lands', 'sun', 'sea' and 'falls'.

Ask the children to write a short rhyming poem (a series of couplets or quatrains) about an animal, a creature, the weather or a person. Here is a delightful poem by Daniel, aged ten:

Dalesman

Old man, smoky beard,
Sunshine smile and haystack hair,
Hands like roots and corn gold skin.
He doesn't have a single care.

Old man, falcon nosed,
Bent old back and raven's eye,
Thin as a scarecrow in his fields,
He stands and sees the world go by.

Some activities for the Literacy Hour

A simple starting point for junior children is to look with the teacher at a poem in the Literacy Hour. It is important not to trawl tediously through, explaining words and phrases before the poem has a chance to 'breath'. Children should be given the opportunity of hearing the full poem read with feeling, reread and appreciated prior to any discussion. With one Year 6 group I looked at a range of poetry over a half term. I wanted to:

- Encourage children to read, prepare and present a selection of poems.
- Encourage the children to share their opinions about the poems.
- Compare a range of poetry and recognise the key differences between prose, poetry, playscript and non-fiction writing.
- Avoid fierce interrogation or lectures – appreciation of the poem comes before analysis.
- Convince the children that there is 'no right answer' when exploring meaning.
- Challenge them to justify their points of view by reference to the text.
- Value each contribution, e.g. 'That's a good point', 'It's interesting you should say that...'
- Use specialist terminology to provide the language for talking about the poem: theme, mood, rhythm, syllable, rhyme, metre, imagery, verse, figures of speech.
- Encourage the children to discuss the language: the choice of particular words and phrases (for example powerful expressive verbs and vivid adjectives), significant detail, repetition, different verse structures (for example to distinguish between rhyming and non-rhyming poetry) and use of punctuation.

Firstly we looked at the poem *Night* by Richard Pasco, which appears in the collection *Lizard Over Ice*, edited by Gervase Phinn and published by Thomas Nelson.

Night

Gently laps the sea.
The black rocks glisten wet.
Moonlight silvers the sand,
And the gulls are quiet.

Night. Ice in the air.
Trees silhouetted, stark, straight.
Branches like ragged birds,
So still, so black.

Beyond the dark rocks
Stretching shingle to the sea,
Patches of blue mud
And pools of silver.

Night. Ice in the water.
Great Neptune sleeps
And in the cold, cold deep,
All is still, all is black.

The children were asked to read the poem quietly to themselves. We then read it slowly together. A general discussion followed:

- What, in one sentence is this poem about?
- What parts do you particularly like? Can you say why?
- What parts don't you understand? Can we see if we can get to the meaning?
- Is there anything else you wish to say about this poem?

These general questions opened up the discussion and from there we focused upon some of the features of this poem: the creation of atmosphere, the four-line stanzas, the lack of rhyme, the gentle quiet rhythm which reflects the tranquillity of the scene, the frequent use of the letter 's' (*sea, silvers, sand, silhouetted, stark, still, stretching, shingle, silver, sleeps*), the contrasting colours, the choice of certain words and phrases, use of significant detail, repetition and figures of speech.

The children were then grouped according to ability for guided reading of some poems, taken from the collections recommended earlier. The material was carefully differentiated so, for example, the most able group was asked to consider a complex free verse poem *Mother to Son* by the American writer Langston Hughes and the least able group to read and study the more accessible *An Accident* by Wes Magee. The groups all had to examine the poems using the question prompts:

- What, in one sentence, do you think this poem is about?
- What parts do you particularly like? Can you say why?
- What parts don't you understand? Can you see if you can get to the meaning?
- Is there anything else you wish to say about this poem?

Another interesting activity to encourage the children to focus upon the structure of the verse and on aspects of the language is the DARTS approach (*Directed Activities Related to Texts*) which involves reorganising, completing or adding to a piece of text. Sometimes words are omitted (cloze procedure), paragraphs reordered (sequencing) or a text broken into instalments (prediction). These techniques encourage the use of a range of reading strategies and can also be used with stories and non-fiction material. Searching for clues in order to complete a piece of text, reordering jumbled sentences, segmenting (marking off key groups of phrases or sentences), labelling, grouping (putting sections of text into different categories) and rewriting the information in the form of tables, diagrams and flow charts, encourages careful reading and develops the children's comprehension skills.

For example, in the first part of the Literacy Hour I worked with a Year 5 group and studied the poem by Adrian Tuplin, aged 12, in which single words and phrases had been omitted. We considered possible alternatives to fill in the spaces and decided on a number of appropriate titles.

The DARTS activity was to complete the following poem:

> The slave ship sails,
> .... the water silently, ...,
> Masts .... in the wind
> And the sails .... and ....
> .... timbers, ... hold,
> Full of the black cargo.
> Crack! the whip cuts the skin
> Of the slaves who dance
> To the music of the ....

Here is our group effort:

> The slave ship sails,
> Softly in the still water, silently, secretly.
> Masts moan in the wind
> And the sails flap and flutter.
> Tired timbers, filthy hold,
> Full of the black cargo.
> Crack! the whip cuts the skin
> Of the slaves who dance
> To the music of the ocean.

Here is the original poem:

> The slave ship sails,
> Cutting the water silently, surely,
> Masts sway in the wind
> And the sails puff and billow.
> Creaking timbers, groaning hold,
> Full of the black cargo.
> Crack! the whip cuts the skin
> Of the slaves who dance
> To the music of the boy's flute.

The children were then grouped according to ability for guided reading. They were asked to look at a range of poems, varying in complexity and with parts omitted. They were asked to discuss the verses and supply appropriate words and phases.

The splendidly amusing poem *Nut Up My Nose* by Irene Rawnsley, which appears in her lively collection *Ask a Silly Question* published by Methuen, was read to and discussed by a Year 5 group. In the playground, Tracy Smith tells John to open his mouth and close his eyes and he will get a big surprise. When he does so, she pushes a nut up his nose and try as he might it will not come down. When he tells his teacher, she orders him to get on with his writing. His mum tries the vacuum cleaner, the nurse tries with a torch and a pair of tweezers but with no success – the nut remains stuck up his nose. Finally, the doctor manages to extract the nut with a long hooked needle and all ends happily. I omitted to read the final verse, where John's mother sends a letter of complaint to school, and asked the children to complete the poem. Here are two very inventive final verses:

> Next day in the playground,
> I found Tracy Smith sitting on a wall.
> 'Look what I've got for you,' I said to her.
> And I pushed the nut up her nose!

> 'Ah, ha,' said the doctor,
> 'What have we here?'
> And before I could say, 'Nut up my nose.'
> There it was in the palm of my hand.
> 'Now then,' said the doctor smiling,
> 'What have you got to say?'
> 'Thanks doctor,' I said – and I ate the nut!

Sequencing is another activity which encourages children to discuss and examine a poem's structure. A Year 4 group was given the following verse (which appears in the collection *Classroom Creatures* by Gervase Phinn) which had been jumbled up. The children were asked to place the lines in an order which made sense and which sounded interesting.

Christmas Presents for Miss
Chocolates in a fancy box –
For the teacher who is tops!
A towel and an oven glove –
From Gemma Thompson with my love.
A bottle stands in thick brown paper –
All the best from Darren Baker.
Perfumed soap from Lee and Chris,
You're our favourite teacher, Miss.
Flowers in a coloured pot –
Happy Christmas, Helen Bott.
A china dog with painted face –
For the teacher who is ace!
And from the nuisance of the class
The Nativity encased in glass.
I know this year I've been a pain,
I'm sorry, Miss – with love from Wayne.

And though she's taught for many years,
The teacher's eyes still fill with tears,
For children know the ones who care
And that is why those gifts are there.

Scaffolding is where the teacher uses a piece of text and encourages the children to model their writing upon it. I used the poem *Ups and Downs* by June Crebbin, which appears in the anthology *The Jungle Sale*, Viking Kestrel, as a focus in the Literacy Hour with a mixed-age Key Stage 2 class. The first verse sets the pattern: six lines beginning in exactly the same way.

> Teachers like you
> to
> sit up
> shut up
> and put your hand up
> when you have something to say.

There follow another four verses describing the sort of things teachers like their pupils to do. I asked the children to write their own version of *Ups and Downs* based upon June Crebbin's amusing poem, but relating what parents like children to do. Here is Rowena's poem:

> Parents like you
> to
> tidy your room
> make your bed
> do your homework
> and come in early.
>
> Parents like you
> to
> brush your teeth
> comb your hair
> wash behind your ears
> and clean your shoes.
>
> Parents like you
> to
> eat your cabbage
> sit up properly
> wash the dishes
> and turn the television off.
>
> Parents like you
> to
> be quiet
> be sensible
> be polite
> and speak nicely.
>
> Parents like you
> to
> behave as they think they did when they were our age!

The short poem, *School Trip* by Peter Dixon, published in the anthology *Big Billy*, Sarsen Press, and one of my own poems of the same title, which appears in *Classroom Creatures*, Roselea Publications, were used as models for poetry writing with a Year 6 group. We discussed the two versions, compared and contrasted the themes, use of words, details and descriptions before a 'guided writing' session. One group produced this very amusing and cleverly-written narrative poem:

> On our school trip...
> Jane Tomlinson stayed too long in the sun,
> And burnt her arms, legs and face,
> And had to stay in hospital
>
> On our school trip...
> William Ellis dropped his purse down a grate,
> And tried to get it back and got his fingers caught,
> And cried for the rest of the day.
>
> On our school trip...
> Mr. Johnson slipped on a rock and fell in the sea.
> Miss Draper tried to grab him and fell in too,
> And her bag disappeared in the weeds.
>
> On our school trip...
> Wayne was sick on Jennifer, who was sick on Jason,
> Who was sick on Wayne,
> And Wayne was sick again.
>
> On our school trip...
> The bus driver hit a car and his wing mirror fell off.
> He shouted and shouted and blamed the teachers
> For not making us sit down.
>
> On our school trip...
> Becky got lost and a policeman brought her back
> And said Miss Draper ought to be more careful,
> Letting children go off by themselves.
>
> I don't think I'll go on the school trip next year.
> It was really, really boring!

The approaches to poetry outlined above bring children and text closer together in the kind of challenging and varied way suggested in the National Literacy Strategy:

> Primary children should, through reading and writing, develop their powers of imagination, inventiveness and critical awareness.
>
> ...Reading is by no means a passive process: it involves searching; problem solving; active prediction; and an ability to bring past knowledge and experience to bear.

(DfEE 1998b)

Chapter 9
Responding to Non-Fiction Texts at Key Stage 1

Throughout the Key Stages children should have the opportunity to read a range of non-fiction texts and learn about the underlying organisational ideas expressed in them. As with fiction and poetry, the teacher will explore with the children in the Literacy Hour, the dynamic relationship between word, sentence and text in non-fiction material, discussing the structural and linguistic features of information texts and encouraging the children to reread, justify a point of view, investigate and reflect. Unlike much of the prose and poetry that children encounter, non-fiction material often contains subject specific vocabulary and more formal, impersonal registers. Some children, therefore, find it difficult and will need additional support.

Over a two week period I presented a series of non-fiction books to infant children in the shared reading sessions. The six short books: Set D in the *Story Chest Stepping Stones, Investigations Series*, are published by Kingscourt. Inspired by children's questions, the texts focus upon a series of environmental themes: *Wind, Rain, Maps, Rubbish, Dinosaurs* and *A Hundred Years Ago*. My aims were to introduce the pupils to a variety of non-fiction material and:

- encourage them to listen attentively in a range of contexts;
- stimulate their own spoken language, encouraging them to speak with clarity, confidence and expression;
- teach them to understand the structure of a non-fiction book and learn about title page, contents, glossary, author information and bibliography;
- help them understand how successful information books work.

The first book we looked at was called *Dinosaurs*. A series of questions are answered throughout a simply-written text, which is enhanced with large colourful drawings. On each page is a question and the answer: 'What were dinosaurs?' 'What were the different kinds?' 'Which was the longest, biggest, smallest, fastest, fiercest?' 'Which was the last of the dinosaurs?' 'Why did the dinosaurs die out?' The children gathered in a half circle on the carpet in the Reading Corner, sitting in a position where they were able to see the book.

- The class was shown the cover of the book. Title page, author and illustrator were introduced.

- I demonstrated how to turn the pages of the book without damaging it.
- A general discussion followed about dinosaurs. The children, not surprisingly, knew a great deal and several could pronounce the different kinds of dinosaur and tell me which were vegetarian and which meat-eaters. Information, names and key words were noted on a chart set out on the whiteboard and the children asked to think about what we needed to find out about these incredible creatures.

What I Already Know *about Dinosaurs*	*What I Would like to Know* *about Dinosaurs*

- The first three pages of the book were read:

> Dinosaurs were creatures which lived on Earth for a long time before there were any people.
> The word 'dinosaur' means terrible lizard.
> There were hundreds of different kinds of dinosaur within two main groups:
> Some walked on two legs. They were very fast.
> They were very fierce and ate other animals.
> One group were the lizard-hipped dinosaurs. Some of these walked on four legs. They were very big and slow.
> They ate plants.

- The text was reread and the pictures, depicting various lizard-hipped dinosaurs such as the Diplodocus and the Dienonychus, were discussed: their shapes, sizes, movements, colours and so on.
- The next three pages were read and the scrutiny of the text repeated.
- The text was finally reread from beginning to end with the children encouraged to join in when they felt confident to do so. They were asked the questions posed in the book to assess their understanding.
- During the final reading the text was interrogated in a sensitive way and used to teach certain skills and decoding strategies. Children were asked to identify words beginning with a particular letter, talk about and spell out the key words, guess what certain words meant, supply alternatives for high frequency words, discuss the use of full stops, commas, exclamation marks, italics, bold type and different font sizes.
- Each child was asked to make a non-fiction booklet with captions.
- A big class mural was made based on the information in the book with cut-out dinosaurs and simple text.

Chapter 10
Responding to Non-Fiction Texts at Key Stage 2

At Key Stage 2 the teacher will develop and extend reading beyond the initial stage of literacy, teaching children the higher order reading skills they will need to cope with increasingly demanding material. Children will be taught the techniques of:

- Skimming: a quick reading of a text to get an initial overall impression.
- Scanning: a careful reading of a text where the reader seeks specific information on a subject.
- Responding: careful reading of the text where the reader responds on the topic in a personal and uncritical way.
- Reflecting: a careful reading of the text where the reader reflects upon the text in an impersonal, critical way.
- Summarising: a careful reading of the text where the reader identifies the salient points and condenses the material.

In the course of their primary years children are likely to come across five main kinds of non-fiction text. All are represented in the suggested 'ten non-fiction books' described earlier:

1. *Retelling events*
   Written in the past tense and in chronological order as in *War Boy: A Country Childhood* by Michael Foreman, Puffin, where the writer recounts his experiences growing up in the Second World War or in *The History of Britain and Ireland* by Christopher Wright, Kingfisher Books, where historical events are retold.
2. *Explaining a process*
   Non-chronological writing in the simple present tense as in *How Your Body Works*, Usborne Books, where the writer explains the functions of the human body or chronological writing in the past tense as in *Keeping Clean: A Very Peculiar History* by Daisy Kerr, Watts Books, where the writer explores ablutions through the ages.
3. *Describing*
   Non-chronological writing in the simple present or past tense as in *World Religions Past and Present*, Moonlight Books, where the writer explores the

core beliefs common to most religions, or in *Anne Frank: Beyond the Diary* by Rudd van der Rol and Rian Verhoeven, Puffin, where the writers describe Anne's life and the frightening world in which she lived.

4. *Instructing*

    Written in the imperative and in chronological order as in the recipes in *Skills Foundation Books* by John Jackman and Wendy Wren, Nelson, where the writer explains how something is done through a series of sequenced stages.

5. *Persuading and discussing*

    Non-chronological writing in the simple present tense as in *Pictures of Home* by Colin Thompson, Julia MacRae, where the writer, through pictures and children's commentaries, presents the case for the happy home or in *The Gaia Atlas of Planet Management*, edited by Norman Myers, where detailed information is given and a forceful argument is presented concerning care of the planet.

I used the non-fiction text *The Brain and the Nervous System* by Brian R. Ward, Franklin Watts, with a Year 5 and 6, mixed-age, mixed-ability group. The book is written in clear accessible language, has well-spaced print and bright, bold, full-colour illustrations, is of manageable length and includes a title page, contents, glossary and index. I wanted to use this shared text to focus upon some key aspects of non-fiction writing:

- The writer's intention: Is he retelling events or explaining a process or describing or instructing or persuading?
- The structure: Examination of how the text is constructed, with discussion of the sentence structures and paragraphing, the purpose and use of punctuation, the page layout.
- The features of information books: *Introduction, Contents, Chapter Headings, Footnotes, Glossary, Index, Bibliography, Author Biography.*
- The language: The choice of words, specialist terminology, use of examples, scientific phrases.
- The drawings and diagrams: How the writer clarifies, explains and illustrates a point by their use.

In one session we analysed the second chapter of the book, *The Spinal Cord*, (about 240 words) in some depth. The chapter begins:

The spinal cord is an extension of the brain, extending about two thirds of the way down the middle of the back to just below the ribs. It is a rod of brain tissue, with a small hole running though it. The whole cord is covered with membranes, just like the brain, and it too is bathed inside and out with protective fluid.

The children were set a series of tasks to develop their critical reading and understanding of the text. By investigative, reflective, discursive rereading and writing activities, I wanted them to explore the text and consolidate the teaching points I had raised in the shared reading sessions. Amongst other things the children were asked to:

- find alternative words for *extension, protective, enclosed, flexibility, fragile, ingenious* and *interlock*;
- identify adjectives and nouns, verbs and adverbs by highlighting them in different colours and note in the text the frequency of each;
- use a dictionary and computer thesaurus to compile a small glossary of the specialist words and phrases which are used in the text (such as *ligament, vertebrae, muscle, skull,* and *nervous system*);
- list the key points about *the spinal cord* gleaned from the chapter;
- devise a set of questions based on the text to test the reader's understanding;
- use other reference books and the computer to collect any additional facts about *the spinal column*;
- read the factsheet, study the illustrations about *the structure of the brain* provided by the teacher and convert the notes into a chapter of prose;
- compare their own version of *the structure of the brain* with the chapter printed in the book;
- read the five paragraphs about *the function of the cortex* which have been cut up, and arrange them in the correct sequence;
- read the chapter on *the cerebrum* in which certain parts have been omitted and provide appropriate words and phrases to fill the spaces.

Three chapters from *The Brain and the Nervous System* were used as a basis for some DARTS activities. A less able group was asked to decide upon the full and correct version of the text when words had been omitted (cloze procedure). Another average ability group was given six jumbled paragraphs and asked to arrange them in what they considered to be the correct order (sequencing). The most able pupils were given more demanding tasks of underlining the main points in the text, segmenting (marking off set groups of sentences) labelling, grouping (putting sections of text into different categories) and representing the information in the form of tables, diagrams and flow charts.

From learning about and discussing non-fiction writing we progressed into guided writing where the children focused on the specific aspects of the writing process. Activities included:

- planning a piece of non-fiction writing;
- converting notes into prose;
- composing a piece of clear informative text;
- expanding and contracting a factual text (elaborating and summarising);
- converting simple to complex and complex to simple sentences;
- connecting points together in an argument;
- composing a piece of persuasive writing;
- editing work for clarity and presentation.

Here is an example. One able group of four Year 6 children was given various jumbled facts about water and asked to compose a simple, readable, clearly-expressed piece of prose.

The facts:

> Plants would die without water.
> We need about 80 litres of water a day to have a reasonable life.
> We have more water than we need.
> Water is not distributed evenly around the world.
> Without water we would die.
> Hospitals and factories need water. So do schools.
> There is flooding in India.
> Average water consumption in USA is 500 litres per person per day.
> Over 97% of water on Earth is salty.
> One person needs at least 5 litres of water a day to survive.
> There is drought in North Africa.
> 3% of the world's water is fresh.
> Water is the liquid of life.
> Consumption of water in Madagascar is 5.4 litres per person per day.
> Rivers, lakes, underground stores hold less than 1% of the world's water.
> Most fresh water is locked away in icecaps.

The Pupils' Prose Version:

Without water we would die! Hospitals, schools, factories, agriculture, homes, everything would stop, because water is essential to keep us alive and everything going. Most of the water in the world is not of any real use to us. Over 97% of water on the Earth is salty and of the remainder most of that is frozen in icecaps. Less than 1% of water is held in rivers, lakes and underground stores.

Despite the very small amount of fresh water available, we have more than enough water for everyone in the world. The problem is that water is not evenly spread throughout the planet and some people have more water than they need whilst others have barely enough to survive. In some parts of the world, like India, there is flooding and in others, as in North Africa, there is severe drought. The average person needs about 80 litres of water a day to live a reasonable life but consumption varies from 500 litres per day in the USA to 5.4 litres in Madagascar.

We must take greater care of our water. It is the liquid of life and should not be taken for granted.

A structured approach for recording and remembering information is note-making and children need to be taught some of the most effective techniques.

• Skim the text to get a first impression.
• Scan the text to locate the main items of information.
• Write main heading in capital letters.
• Write section headings clearly and underline.
• Indent sub-headings.
• Indent again for examples or points which you want to develop.
• Leave space between sections in case you need to add information later.
• Do not use full stops and commas.
• Use numbers to list points in order of importance – 1(a)i, 2(b)ii, 3(c)iii

- Use symbols and abbreviations – therefore (.˙.), because (˙.˙), note well (N.B.), example (e.g.), that is (i.e.), equal (=), and (&), etc., asterisks (*), arrows (> < ∧).
- Use capitals and colours to emphasise.

Here is an example composed by a group of Year 6 children using the earlier piece of text.

WATER

The World's Water
97% of water on Earth is salty
3% of water on Earth is fresh
    – rivers, lakes, underground stores hold less than 1% of world's fresh water
    – most fresh water locked away in icecaps
Water is not distributed evenly around the world.
    – There is flooding in *India.*
    – There is drought in *North Africa*
Why do we need water?
Water is the liquid of life – we need it to live
Without water:
    plants would die
    hospitals + factories + schools would stop
How much water do we need?
We have more water than we need
We need about 80 litres of water a day to *have a reasonable life*
One person needs at least 5 litres of water a day *to survive*
Average water consumption varies around the world
    USA = 500 litres per person per day
    Madagascar = 5.4 litres per person per day

Conclusion

The National Curriculum and the National Literacy Strategy both stress the vital importance of providing rich and stimulating texts – fiction, poetry, playscripts and non-fiction material. All pupils are entitled to hear, read and discuss picture books, nursery rhymes, folk tales, legends and other stories in different genres, to be exposed to literature which will challenge and excite them and to learn, through lively discussion and sensitive analysis of the texts, just how language works.

Children should:

> Encounter an environment in which they are surrounded by books and other reading material, presented in an attractive and inviting way. Activities should ensure that pupils hear books, stories and poems read aloud . . . as well as rhymes, poems, songs and familiar stories (including traditional stories from a variety of cultures).
>
> (DES 1989)

If we provide children with this variety of stimulating texts, with stories and poems that fascinate, excite, intrigue and amuse, that give them fresh insights, that open their minds and imaginations and that introduce them to the wonderful richness and range of language, then we produce avid, enthusiastic and discriminating readers and offer them the very best models for their own writing. This is no new philosophy. It has been a fundamental belief of all those who have attempted to open the wonderful world of literature and language to the young. John Locke wrote over 300 years ago:

> When he can talk 'tis time he should begin to learn to read, but as to this, give me leave here to inculcate again what is very apt to be forgotten, namely that great care is to be taken that it be never made as a business to him nor he look upon it as a task. Their being forced and tied down to their books in an age at enmity with all such restraint, has I doubt not been reason why a great many have hated books and learning all their lives after. It is like a surfeit which leaves an aversion to learning not to be removed. Thus much for learning to read, which let him never be driven to nor chid for: cheat him into it if you can, but make it not a business for him. 'Tis better it be a year later before he can read than that

he should this way get an aversion to learning. Use your skill to make his will supple and pliant to reason. Teach him to love credit and commendation, to abhor being thought ill or meanly of, especially by you and his mother, and then the rest will come all easily. When by these easy ways he begins to read, some easy pleasant book suited to his capacity should be put into his hands wherein the entertainment might draw him on and reward his pains in reading.

As Goethe said: 'Everything has been thought of before. Our challenge is to think of it again.'

Endpiece

Reading Round the Class

On Friday we have reading round the class.
Kimberley Bloomer is the best.
She sails slowly along the page like a great galleon
And everyone looks up and listens.
'Beautiful reading, Kimberley, dear,' sighs Mrs Scott,
'And with such fluency, such feeling.
It's a delight to hear...'

On Friday we have reading round the class.
I'm the worst.
I stumble and mumble along slowly like a broken down train
And everyone looks up and listens.
Then they smile and snigger and whisper behind their hands.
'Dear me,' sighs Mrs Scott, 'rather rusty Simon.
Quite a bit of practice needed, don't you think?
Too much television and football, that's your trouble,
And not enough reading.'

Is it any wonder that I hate books!

Gervase Phinn

Bibliography

Arnold, M. (1890) *Reports on Elementary Schools, 1852–1882*. London: Macmillan.

Barber, M. (1998) 'Transforming standards in literacy', in McClelland, N. (ed.) *Building a Literate Nation*. London: Trentham Books.

Barnes, D. and Egford, R. F. (eds) (1973) *Twentieth Century Short Stories*. London: Harrap.

Beard, R. (1991) *Developing Reading, 3–13*. London: Hodder and Stoughton.

Bennett, J. (1982) *A Choice of Stories*. Swindon: The School Library Association.

Bettelheim, B. and Zelan, K. (1982) *On Learning to Read: The Child's Fascination with Meaning*. London: Thames and Hudson.

Blunkett, D. (1999) *The Times*, Friday, 23 July, 1999.

Bragg, M. (1983) 'Introduction' in *How to Teach Poetry*. Scannell, V. Loughton: Piatkus Press.

Burman, C. (1990) 'Organising for reading' in Wade, B. (ed.) *Reading for Real*. Milton Keynes: Open University Press.

Causley, C. (1990) *The Puffin Book of Magic Verse*. London: Penguin Books.

Clark, M. (1976) *Young Fluent Readers*. London: Heinemann.

Colwell, E. (1991) *Story Telling*. Stroud: Thimble Press.

DES (1967) *Children and their Primary Schools (The Plowden Report)*. London: HMSO.

DES (1975) *A Language for Life (The Bullock Report)*. London: HMSO.

DES (1984) *English 5–16*. London: HMSO.

DES (1987) *Teaching Poetry in the Secondary School*. London: HMSO.

DES (1988a) *The Report of the Committee of Inquiry into the Teaching of English Language (The Kingman Report)*. London: HMSO.

DES (1988b) *The National Curriculum Proposals for English for Ages 5–11 (The Cox Report)*. London: HMSO.

DES (1989) *English in the National Curriculum, Programme of Study for Reading at Key Stage 1*. London: HMSO.

DES (1990a) *English in the National Curriculum*. London: HMSO.

DES (1990b) *The Teaching and Learning of Reading in Primary Schools*. London: HMSO.

DfEE (1998a) *National Year of Reading: Getting Ready*. London: DfEE Press.

DfEE (1998b) *The National Literacy Strategy: The Management of Literacy at School Level.* London: DfEE Press.

Graham, J. and Placket, E. (1982) *Developing Readers.* Swindon: School Library Association.

Holmes, R. (1990). *Coleridge: Early Visions.* London: Hodder and Stoughton.

Hutchinson, P. *et al.* (1991) *The Story Chest Teachers' File.* Walton-on-Thames: Thomas Nelson.

Hynds, J. (1988) Quoted in Waterland, L. *Read With Me.* Stroud: Thimble Press.

Jones, A. and Buttrey, J. (1970) *Children and Stories.* Oxford: Basil Blackwell.

Landsberg, M. (1990) *The World of Children's Books: A Guide to Choosing the Best.* Hemel Hempstead: Simon and Schuster.

Lewis, C. S. (1977) Quoted in Meek, M. *et al., The Cool Web: The Pattern of Children's Reading.* London: The Bodley Head.

Marum, E. (ed.) (1995). *Towards 2000: The Future of Childhood, Literacy and Schooling.* London: The Falmer Press.

Meek, M. (1970) *How Texts Teach What Readers Learn.* Stroud: Thimble Press.

Meek, M. *et al.* (1977) *The Cool Web: The Pattern of Children's Reading.* London: The Bodley Head.

Meek, M. (1982) *Learning to Read.* London: Bodley Head.

Neate, B. (ed.) (1996) *Literacy Saves Lives.* Shepreth: The United Kingdon Reading Association Press.

Newman, J. ((1984) *The Craft of Children's Writing.* London: Scholastic.

O'Connor, M. (1990) *How to Help Your Child Through School.* London: Harrap.

Phinn, G. (1986) 'Fiction in the classroom', in Blatchford, R. (ed.) *The English Teacher's Handbook.* London: Hutchinson.

Phinn, G. (1987a) 'No language to speak of? Children talking and writing', in Booth, T. *et al.* (ed.) *Preventing Difficulties in Learning: Curricula for All.* Oxford: Basil Blackwell.

Phinn, G. (1987b) *The Vital Resource: Poetry in the Primary School.* Huddersfield: Woodfield and Stanley Ltd.

Phinn, G. (1988) *Touches of Beauty: Teaching Poetry.* Doncaster: Roselea Publications.

Phinn, G. (1992) 'Choosing books for young readers: habituated to the vast', in Harrison, C. and Coles, M. (eds) *The Reading for Real Handbook.* London: Routledge.

Shilling, J. (1999) 'Creating an appetite for adventure', in the *Daily Telegraph,* Saturday 24 July 1999.

Tucker, N. (1982) *The Child and the Book: A Psychological and Literary Exploration.* Cambridge: Cambridge University Press.

Waterland, L. (ed.) (1988) *Read With Me: An Apprenticeship Approach to Reading.* Stroud: Thimble Press.

Index

3285771?

The Camel's Hump
and other poems

Compiled by Tig Thomas

Miles
KelLY

First published in 2010 by Miles Kelly Publishing Ltd
Harding's Barn, Bardfield End Green, Thaxted, Essex, CM6 3PX, UK

2 4 6 8 10 9 7 5 3 1

Editorial Director Belinda Gallagher

Art Director Jo Cowan

Assistant Editor Claire Philip

Designer Joe Jones

Junior Designer Kayleigh Allen

Production Manager Elizabeth Collins

Reprographics Stephan Davis, Ian Paulyn

ISBN 978-1-84810-369-6

Printed in China

British Library Cataloguing-in-Publication Data
A catalogue record for this book is available from the British Library

ACKNOWLEDGEMENTS

The publishers would like to thank Kirsten Wilson for
the illustrations she contributed to this book.

All other artwork from the Miles Kelly Artwork Bank

Made with paper from a sustainable forest

www.mileskelly.net
info@mileskelly.net

www.factsforprojects.com

Self-publish your
children's book

buddingpress.co.uk

Contents

An Alphabet of People

A is for Alfred, who Angled at Ayr,

B is for Bernard, who Baited a Bear,

C is for Clara, who Came with her Chum,

D is for Donald, who Danced on his Drum,

E is for Eve, who Encountered an Eel,

F is for Fanny, who Fashioned a Frill,

G is for George, who has Gone to the Glen,

H is for Harold, who Hustled the Hen,

I is for Irene, who Intends to use Ink,

J is for Joseph, who Jumped a high Jink,

K is for Kenneth, who Kept a large Kite,

L is for Lawrence, who Laughed at the Light,

M is for Malcolm, who Marched to the Mine,

N is for Norman, of Newts he caught Nine,

O is for Oswald, who an Owl did Observe,

P is for Peggy, with a Pot of Preserve,

Q is for Quentin, who Questioned a Quail,

R is for Robert, who Rests on a Rail,

S is for Susan, whose Steed lost a Shoe,

T is for Thomas, who Tried to Tattoo,

U is for Ursula, who Upset an Urn,

V is for Victor, with Volumes by Verne,

W is for William, who Went to the Well,

X is for Xavier, who eXpects to eXcel,

Y is for Yorick, a Youth who can Yell,

Z is for Zeno, a Zulu with Zeal.

Anonymous

The Duck and the Kangaroo

Said the Duck to the Kangaroo,
"Good gracious! How you hop!
Over the fields and the water too,
As if you never would stop!
My life is a bore in this nasty pond,
And I long to go out in the world beyond!
I wish I could hop like you!"
Said the Duck to the Kangaroo.

"Please give me a ride on your back!"
Said the Duck to the Kangaroo.
"I would sit quite still, and say nothing but 'Quack,'
The whole of the long day through!
And we'd go to the Dee, and the Jelly Bo Lee,
Over the land, and over the sea;
Please take me a ride! O do!"
Said the Duck to the Kangaroo.

Said the Kangaroo to the Duck.
"This requires a little reflection;
Perhaps on the whole it might bring me luck,
And there seems but one objection,
Which is, if you'll let me speak so bold,
Your feet are unpleasantly wet and cold,
And would probably give me the roo-
Matiz!" said the Kangaroo.

Said the Duck, "As I sat on the rocks,
I have thought over that completely,
And I bought four pair of worsted socks
Which fit my web-feet neatly.
And to keep out the cold I've bought a cloak,
And every day a cigar I'll smoke,
All to follow my own dear true
Love of a Kangaroo!"

Said the Kangaroo, "I'm ready!
All in the moonlight pale,
But to balance me well, dear Duck, sit steady!
And quite at the end of my tail!"
So away they went with a hop and a bound,
And they hopped the whole world three time round;
And who so happy, O who,
As the Duck and the Kangaroo?

Edward Lear

Arabella Miller

Little Arabella Miller
Had a fuzzy caterpillar.
First it climbed upon her mother,
Then upon her baby brother.
They said, "Arabella Miller,
Put away your caterpillar!"

Anonymous

9

My Serving Men

I keep six honest serving-men
(They taught me all I knew);
Their names are **What** and **Why** and **When**
And **How** and **Where** and **Who**.
I send them over land and sea,
I send them east and west;
But after they have worked for me,
I give them all a rest.

I let them rest from nine till five,
For I am busy then,
As well as breakfast, lunch, and tea,
For they are hungry men.
But different folk have different views;
I know a person small —
She keeps ten million serving-men,
Who get no rest at all!

She sends 'em abroad on her own affairs,
From the second she opens her eyes –
One million Hows, two million Wheres,
And seven million Whys!

Rudyard Kipling

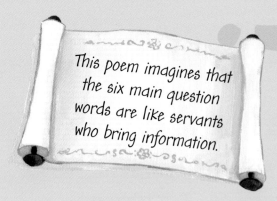

This poem imagines that the six main question words are like servants who bring information.

I Can't Remember

Do you love me,
Or do you not?
You told me once,
But I forgot.

Anonymous

From *Wild Swans at Coole*

The trees are in their autumn beauty,
The woodland paths are dry,
Under the October twilight the water
Mirrors a still sky;
Upon the brimming water among the stones
Are nine-and-fifty Swans.

W B Yeats

Swan

Swan swam over the sea;
Swim, swan, swim.
Swan swam back again;
Well swum swan.

Anonymous

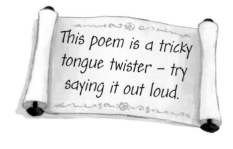

This poem is a tricky tongue twister – try saying it out loud.

From A Boy's Aspirations

I was four yesterday – when I'm quite old,
I'll have a cricket-ball made of pure gold;
I'll carve the roast meat, and help soup and fish;
I'll get my feet wet whenever I wish;

I'll spend a hundred pounds every day;
I'll have the alphabet quite done away;
I'll have a parrot without a sharp beak;
I'll see a pantomime six times a week;

I'll have a rose-tree, always in bloom;
I'll keep a dancing bear in Mamma's room;
I'll spoil my best clothes, and not care a pin;
I'll have no visitors ever let in;

I'll never stand up to show that I'm grown;
No one shall say to me, "Don't throw a stone!"
I'll drop my butter'd toast on the new chintz;
I'll have no governess giving her hints.

I'll have a nursery up in the stars;
I'll lean through windows without any bars;
I'll sail without my nurse in a big boat;
I'll have no comforters tied round my throat;

I'll have a language with not a word spell'd;
I'll ride on horseback without being held;
I'll hear Mamma say, "My boy, good as gold!"
When I'm a grown-up man sixty years old.

Menella Bute Smedley

A Boy's Song

Where the pools are bright and deep,
Where the grey trout lies asleep,
Up the river and over the lea,
That's the way for Billy and me.

Where the blackbird sings the latest,
Where the hawthorn blooms the
   sweetest,
Where the nestlings chirp and flee,
That's the way for Billy and me.

Where the mowers mow the cleanest,
Where the hay lies thick and greenest,
There to track the homeward bee,
That's the way for Billy and me.

Lea meadow

16

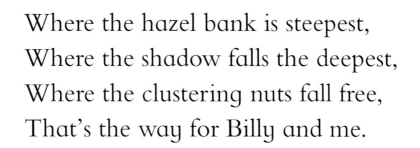

Where the hazel bank is steepest,
Where the shadow falls the deepest,
Where the clustering nuts fall free,
That's the way for Billy and me.

Why the boys should drive away
Little sweet maidens from their play,
Or love to banter and fight so well,
That's the thing I never could tell.

But this I know, I love to play
Through the meadow, among the hay;
Up the water and over the lea,
That's the way for Billy and me.

James Hogg

Rose and the Lily

Rose dreamed she was a lily,
Lily dreamed she was a rose;
Robin dreamed he was a sparrow;
What the owl dreamed no one knows.

But they all woke up together
As happy as could be.
Said each: "You're lovely, neighbour,
But I'm very glad I'm me."

Anonymous

From *One and One*

Two little girls are better than one
Two little boys can double the fun,
Two little birds can build a fine nest,
Two little arms can love mother best.
Two little ponies must go to a span;
Two little pockets has my little man;
Two little eyes to open and close,
Two little ears and one little nose,
Two little elbows, dimpled and sweet,
Two little shoes on two little feet,
Two little lips and one little chin,
Two little cheeks with a rose shut in;
Two little shoulders, chubby and strong,
Two little legs running all day long.

Mary Mapes Dodge

A Little Song of Life

Glad that I live am I;
That the sky is blue;
Glad for the country lanes,
And the fall of dew.

After the sun the rain;
After the rain the sun;
This is the way of life,
Till the work be done.

All that we need to do,
Be we low or high,
Is to see that we grow
Nearer the sky.

Lizette Woodworth Reese

The Sun

I told the sun that I was glad,
I'm sure I don't know why;
Somehow the pleasant way he had
Of shining in the sky,
Just put a notion in my head
That wouldn't it be fun.
If, walking on the hill, I said
"I'm happy" to the sun.

John Drinkwater

The Camel's Hump

The camel's hump is an ugly lump
Which well you may see at the Zoo;
But uglier yet is the hump we get
From having too little to do.

Kiddies and grown-ups too-oo-oo,
If we haven't enough to do-oo-oo,
We get the hump

Cameelious hump

The hump that is black and blue

We climb out of bed with a frouzly head
And a snarly-yarly voice;
We shiver and scowl, and we grunt and we growl
At our bath and our boots and our toys;

And there ought to be a corner for me
(And I know there is one for you)
When we get the hump

Cameelious hump

The hump that is black and blue!

The cure for this ill is not to sit still,
Or frowst with a book by the fire;
But to take a large hoe and a shovel also,
And dig till you gently perspire;

And then you will find that the sun and the wind,
And the Djinn of the Garden too,
Have lifted the hump
The horrible hump
The hump that is black and blue

I get it as well as you-oo-oo
If I haven't enough to do-oo-oo,
We all get the hump

Cameelious hump

Kiddies and grown-ups too!

Rudyard Kipling

This poem is from one of Kipling's Just So stories, which explains how camels got their humps. Being cross is often described as 'getting the hump'.

Seven Times One

There's no dew left on the daisies and clover
There's no rain left in heaven:
I've said my 'seven times' over and over,
Seven times one are seven.

I am old, so old, I can write a letter;
My birthday lessons are done;
The lambs play always, they know no better;
They are only one times one.

O moon! In the night I have seen you sailing
And shining so round and low;
You were bright! Ah, bright! But your light is failing, –
You are nothing now but a bow.

You moon, have you done something wrong in heaven
That God has hidden your face?

I hope if you have you will soon be forgiven,
And shine again in your place.

O velvet bee, you're a dusty fellow,
You've powdered your legs with gold!
O brave marsh marybuds, rich and yellow,
Give me your money to hold!

O columbine, open your folded wrapper,
Where two twin turtledoves dwell
O cuckoopint, toll me the purple clapper,
That hangs in your clear green bell!

And show me your nest with the young ones in it
I will not steal them away;
I am old! You may trust me, linnet, linnet –
I am seven times one today.

Jean Ingelow

Apples

An apple a day
Sends the doctor away
Apple in the morning
Doctor's warning
Roast apple at night
Starves the doctor outright
Eat an apple going to bed
Knock the doctor on the head

Anonymous

At the Zoo

First I saw the white bear, then I saw the black;
Then I saw the camel with a hump upon his back;
Then I saw the grey wolf, with mutton in his maw;
Then I saw the wombat waddle in the straw;
     Then I saw the elephant a-waving of his trunk;
     Then I saw the monkeys – mercy, how
          unpleasantly they—smelt!

William Makepeace Thackeray

Maw *mouth*

The Use and Abuse of Toads

As into the garden Elizabeth ran
Pursued by the just indignation of Ann,
She trod on an object that lay in her road,
She trod on an object that looked like a toad.
It looked like a toad, and it looked so because
A toad was the actual object it was;
And after supporting Elizabeth's tread
It looked like a toad that was visibly dead.
Elizabeth, leaving her footprint behind,
Continued her flight on the wings of the wind,
And Ann in her anger was heard to arrive
At the toad that was not any longer alive.

She was heard to arrive, for the firmament rang
With the sound of a scream and the noise of a bang,
As her breath on the breezes she broadly bestowed
And fainted away on Elizabeth's toad.
Elizabeth, saved by the sole of her boot,
Escaped her insensible sister's pursuit;
And if ever hereafter she irritates Ann,
She will tread on a toad if she possibly can.

A E Housman

Firmament sky
Insensible unconscious

Dog Problems

Our dog Fred
Et the bread.

Our dog Dash
Et the hash.

Our dog Pete
Et the meat.

Our dog Davy
Et the gravy.

Our dog Toffee
Et the coffee.

Our dog Jake
Et the cake.

Our dog Trip
Et the dip.

And – the worst,
From the first, –

Our dog Fido
Et the pie-dough.

James Whitcomb Riley

33

Jelly

Jelly on the plate
Jelly on the plate

Wibble wobble
Wibble wobble

Jelly on the plate

Anonymous

Ice Cream

I scream,
You scream.
We all scream,
For Ice Cream!

Anonymous

Chopping up Food

Chop chop choppitty chop
Chop off the bottom and chop off the top
What there is left we will put in the pot.

Anonymous

The Story of Fidgety Philip

Let me see if Philip can
Be a little gentleman
Let me see, if he is able
To sit still for once at table:
Thus Papa bade Phil behave;
And Mamma look'd very grave.
But fidgety Phil,
He won't sit still;
He wriggles
and giggles,
And then, I declare
Swings backwards and forwards
And tilts up his chair,
Just like any rocking horse –
"Philip! I am getting cross!"

See the naughty restless child
Growing still more rude and wild.
Till his chair falls over quite.
Philip screams with all his might.

Catches at the cloth, but then
That makes matters worse again.
Down upon the ground they fall.
Glasses, plates, knives, forks and all.

How Mamma did fret and frown.
When she saw them tumbling down!
And Papa made such a face!
Philip is in sad disgrace.

Where is Philip, where is he?
Fairly cover'd up you see!
Cloth and all are lying on him;
He has pull'd down all upon him.
What a terrible to-do!
Dishes, glasses, snapt in two!
Here a knife, and there a fork!
Philip, this is cruel work.
Table all so bare, and ah!
Poor Papa, and poor Mamma
Look quite cross, and wonder how
They shall make their dinner now.

Heinrich Hoffmann

A Gustatory Achievement

Last Thanksgivin'-dinner we
Et at Granny's house, an' she
Had – ist like she alluz does –
Most an' best pies ever wuz.

Canned black burry-pie an' goose
Burry, squshin'-full o' juice;
An' rozburry – yes, an' plum –
Yes, an' churry-pie – um-yum!

Peach an' punkin, too, you bet.
Lawzy! I kin taste 'em yet!
Yes, an' custard-pie, an' mince!

An' – I – ain't – et – no –
pie – since!

James Whitcomb Riley

The person in this poem is remembering a Thanksgiving dinner, the feast Americans celebrate in November.

Index of First Lines